ON THE
IMPENDING BENGAL FAMINE

ON THE

IMPENDING BENGAL FAMINE:

HOW IT WILL BE MET

AND

HOW TO PREVENT FUTURE FAMINES IN INDIA.

BY

SIR H. BARTLE E. FRERE,

G.C.S.I., K.C.B., D.C.L.

GYAN

Published by

Gyan Publishing House
5, Ansari Road
Daryaganj, New Delhi-110002
Phone: 011-47034999, 9811692060
E-mail: books@gyanbooks.com

Distribution Network
gyanbooks.com
India, USA, Canada, UK, Australia

ISBN: 978-93-6208-263-3 (PB)
First Published, 1874

2nd Impression 2024

Printed at: Gyan Press, Delhi.

ON THE IMPENDING BENGAL FAMINE
Author: H. BARTLE E. FRERE

ON THE

IMPENDING BENGAL FAMINE.

ON THE

IMPENDING BENGAL FAMINE:

HOW IT WILL BE MET

AND

HOW TO PREVENT FUTURE FAMINES IN INDIA.

A LECTURE DELIVERED BEFORE THE SOCIETY OF ARTS, DEC. 12, 1873.

BY THE RIGHT HON.

SIR H. BARTLE E. FRERE,

G.C.S.I., K.C.B., D.C.L.,

MEMBER OF THE INDIAN COUNCIL, AND PRESIDENT OF THE ROYAL GEOGRAPHICAL SOCIETY.

WITH THREE MAPS.

LONDON:

JOHN MURRAY, ALBEMARLE STREET;

AND

HENRY S. KING & CO., CORNHILL.

1874.

TABLE OF CONTENTS.

LIST OF ILLUSTRATIONS.

INTRODUCTION.

THE substance of the following pages was addressed as a Lecture to the Society of Arts on the 12th December, 1873, when very gloomy anticipations of impending famine in Bengal were justified by deficiency and irregularity in the usual rainfall.

The subject is one of permanent importance to the largest and richest of our Indian provinces, and indeed to the whole of India. I have therefore made some additions to the original address, including three maps, for which I am indebted to Mr. Trelawny Saunders.

Map I. (facing the Title) shows the position of India with relation to the principal grain-producing countries of the East, andits connection with the markets of the world by various lines of steam communication.

The second (p. 51) shows the various provinces and great administrative divisions of India, and the lines of railway. An outline of Great Britain on the same scale in the margin, affords a means of comparison between the Indian areas and distances, and those to which we are most accustomed in this country.

The third (at the end), the map of Bengal, gives the main divisions of that province, with their areas and population. An outline of Ireland to the same scale will give some help in comparing the calamity apprehended in Bengal with the last great famine of which we have had experience in these islands, as caused by a failure of the usual crops.

I have not made any alterations in the Lecture as originally delivered, merely on account of any subsequent changes in the prospects of the season. One great object of the Lecture was to show that famines are entirely preventible in India, as elsewhere; and the interest of any discussion of means whereby famines may be rendered almost impossible is scarcely lessened even should our best hopes be fulfilled,—should it prove that famine will not occasion the deaths from starvation of such numbers as we feared, and that multitudes may be saved by a timely fall of rain. Even the threat of such a calamity impending for weeks together is a terrible evil, and no pains or expenditure can be misapplied to insure the country against its recurrence.

I have only to add that my remarks can claim no official sanction. The facts are open to all who have studied the subject either practically or from published records. The opinions are those of the Lecturer. The only points on which I feel sure of the concurrence of all authorities in this country are, the anxiety with which they watch the progress of events in India, their entire confidence in the energy and ability of the Viceroy and his able Lieutenants, and their determination that no expense or pains shall be spared to mitigate or avert the evils which threaten the population of Bengal.

22 *Prince's Gardens, London,*
December, 1873.

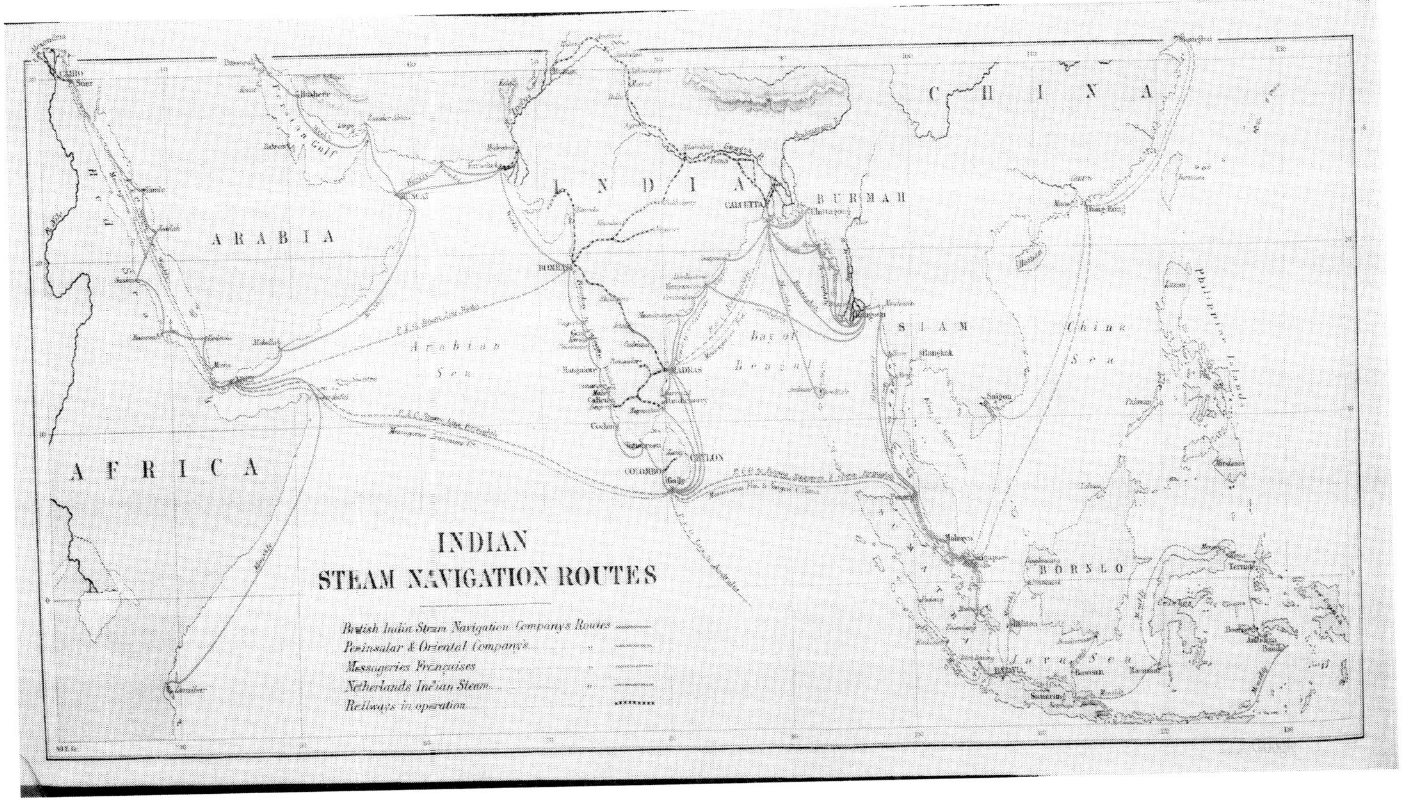
INDIAN
STEAM NAVIGATION ROUTES
British Indian Steam Navigation Company's Routes
Peninsular & Oriental Company's
Messageries Françaises
Netherlands Indian Steam
Railways in operation
AFRICA
ARABIA
INDIA
BURMAH
SIAM
CHINA
BORNEO
Persian Gulf
Arabian Sea
Bay of Bengal
China Sea
Java Sea
Philippine Islands
BOMBAY
MADRAS
CALCUTTA
CEYLON
COLOMBO
BATAVIA
Cochin
Suez
Zanzibar
Bangkok
Saigon
Hong Kong
Shanghai
Luzon
Mindanao
Ternate

ON THE

IMPENDING BENGAL FAMINE.

It is not now proposed to attempt anything like a history of Indian famines. The subject is one of the greatest interest, and there are ample materials for a series of most instructive historical papers, as will be seen by reference to the Reports and Blue Books noted below,* which are only a few of the many which might be mentioned. Neither will I attempt an essay on famines in general. My object is a purely practical one—to describe the mode in which, as far as we can now see, the impending famine in Bengal must be met, and to consider how such calamities may be prevented in future.

Limited scope of present paper.

I.

There are, however, some historical facts which should be borne in mind, for they will be found to have a special bearing upon what we shall have to consider hereafter.

Historical facts to be noted.

* Col. Baird Smith's "Reports on the Famine in the N.W. Provinces." Presented to Parliament, 12th Feb., 1862.

"Papers regarding the Orissa Famine." Presented to Parliament, 1867. Parts I., II., III.

"Supplementary Papers relating to Madras," 30th July, 1867.

See also Hunter's "Rural Bengal," 1868, and the same Author's "Orissa," and "Famine Aspects of Bengal," 1873.

These facts are:—1st, that years of famine or of scarcity rarely come singly; they generally occur in cycles now, as they did of old. The causes and laws of the periodical recurrence of seasons when, the usual rains being deficient or irregular, scarcity and famine ensue, are matters which it would be most important to have fully investigated; but at present we can only note the fact that the recent failure of the periodical rains and consequent threatening of famine may be the crisis, or it may be the end, of such a cycle; but we must also be prepared for its only being the beginning, and no human being can confidently anticipate that the present year of deficient and irregular rainfall may not be followed by worse seasons hereafter.

1st. Famine years and years of scarcity rarely occur singly.

The second historical fact to be noticed, because of its present bearing on our question, is that famines, though they have become much more rare and less severe of late years in India, are by no means of unusual occurrence there or in any other country of Asia. In one or other part of that continent annually during the past forty years famine might be seen either approaching, scourging, or departing from, a large area, and from tens of thousands of practically helpless people; and, so far as we can at present judge, though we may yearly do much to mitigate the pressure, and circumscribe the area of scarcity and famine, it will take years of persistent, well-directed labour before India can be pronounced as secure from the results of scarcity and famine as most parts of Europe.

2nd historical fact. Famines not of rare occurrence in Asia.

The third historical fact to be noted is that, though from the general fertility of the soil, and regularity of the rains, famines are not of such frequent occurrence in

Bengal as elsewhere in India; still when they do occur, they are, partly from the character of the people, and partly from the very infrequency of scarcity, more severe. We know of few things in modern history so terrible in its way as the famine which occurred in Bengal rather more than a century ago; some of the causes which made it so desolating still exist, and some, such as the character and habits of the people, it will perhaps take centuries more to alter.

3rd fact. Famines less frequent in Bengal than in other parts of India, but more severe when they do occur.

I will not attempt to stir your sympathies by vivid descriptions of what occurs in a famine-stricken district. Once seen, the horrors of a real famine can never be effaced from the memory of an eye-witness, and no description can convey anything like an adequate idea of its miseries. Exaggeration is simply impossible, and, if you take the most vivid accounts which have been written by many able writers in the public press, even since this last threatening of famine in Bengal, you will fail to realise what we may fear will be matters of daily occurrence should the present apprehensions regarding a great famine in Bengal be realised.

But there is one more fact which you will find noted in all accurate descriptions of famine, which, like the historical facts already mentioned, should be borne in mind as of importance to right conclusions. It is that men are death-stricken by famine long before they die. The effects of insufficient food long continued may shorten life after a period of some years, or it may be of months or days. But invariably there is a point which is often reached long before death actually ensues, when not even the tenderest care and most scientific nursing can restore

4th historical fact. Mortality from starvation continues long after actual want of food, has been supplied.

a sufficiency of vital energy to enable the sufferer to regain even apparent temporary health and strength. Add to this that the consequences of famine, in death from fevers and epidemics of various kinds, are apt to be quite as fatal as the effects of famine itself. Beyond this, I will say nothing in the way of historical reference or of description, but proceed at once to the main question before us.

We all know that here, even in populous, wealthy London, with hundreds of people, who are able and willing to save any starving fellow-creature, absolutely within call of the sufferer, people do die singly of famine, and in greater numbers more or less slowly of gradual starvation. In fact, if all deaths could be traced to their true cause, insufficiency of nourishment would probably be found to be a very common cause of shortened life in most of the poorer localities in every large city in Europe. With us, the calamity is, in its severest aspects, solitary and occasional; but a knowledge that it does occur suggests the question, why do men die by thousands and millions of want of nourishment in Asia, and in some of the less civilised portions of Europe, and now only singly and rarely in England? though history tells us that at no very distant period famine used to cause the death of thousands here in England also.

II.

Main object of inquiry, why is death from want of food, so much more frequent in India than in England?

Let us trace the causes of the existing differences between our own continent and the East, taking as our examples England as one of the countries of Europe at present best protected against famine, and India as the country of Asia of which we know most, and in which we are most interested.

A great famine, we all know, is caused in India by a general failure of the usual crops, occasioned sometimes by want of, or irregularity in, the periodical rains, aggravated not unfrequently by such causes as floods and wars. These causes, with the exception happily of the last, are not unknown in our own country. Why does irregularity of seasons occasion no universal failure of crops with us here in Europe? Why does a general failure of any great crop cause comparatively little scarcity, and not necessarily any deaths in England? In answering this question we will contrast, step by step, the different conditions of India and of England.

No single cause can be assigned.

But let us first note and remember, throughout our discussion, that you will find nothing like a single cause, but many very complicated causes which account for the immunity of England, and the liability of Asia to famine.

Among the causes are—1st cause. Superior agriculture of England.

(1.) The first great cause of the immunity of England from actual famine, which I would mention, is the greatly improved character of our modern agriculture. In England, however unfavourable the season, a great crop does not often *entirely* and universally fail, partly because we have a great natural variety of soil and climate, partly because of late years we have greatly improved the cultivation of every great crop, so as to render it less liable to failure from natural variation of season.

We have also everywhere not only an improved, but also a more varied agriculture than of old. If grain is a short crop, roots make up the deficiency, or perhaps the hay pays the farmer's rent, and shorter crops sometimes give even better returns than the more abundant, owing to enhanced prices.

Then we have infinitely more capital invested in agriculture than our forefathers, and more intelligence in using it. If grain is scarce, and there is a superabundance of pasture, cattle are imported to eat the grass and make up for the grain. If one sowing of turnips fail, a second and a third sowing is tried. If all crops, in a very bad year, are more or less failures, some are better than others, and, in the general consequent rise in the prices of food, help the farmer to pay his rent. In the worst of times he has a great amount of stock and implements, and of credit. No calamity, such as we are anticipating, can overtake him which does not overtake hundreds of his neighbours. There is general forbearance, and the resources of the whole agricultural community, in credit as well as in capital, stock, and implements, being very large, even a cycle of bad years, though it may ruin many farmers and reduce many agricultural labourers to distress, does not necessarily starve any one. In all these respects England is much better off than Asia.

In many parts of India and China, I have no doubt you could see fields which are as well, if not better cultivated than you could now see in the generality of English fields; and you may find particular agricultural communities who have as good and varied agriculture, as much capital invested, as good credit, stock and implements, as good manures, as any you could find within a hundred miles of London. But, while the improved and various agriculture of England is generally diffused over the whole of the three kingdoms, in Asia you will find the advanced agricultural communities comparatively small and isolated. I say "comparatively," because in India a few hundred miles of excellent farming and cultivation make but a very small spot upon the general map, and you will find all the advanced agricultural communities are more or less isolated by vast extents either of inferior cultivation, or, in many cases, of pathless forests. Thus the beautiful rice, sugar, indigo and opium cultivation of the best districts in Bengal will be found not far removed from vast tracts of deadly Terai forest, or of unreclaimed Soondurbund, Assam, or Central Indian jungle. Some of the best cultivation in the North-West Provinces, the Punjab, Guzerat, and Southern India, where you may see fields and farming communities quite equal in their way to the best in Europe, are frequently within sight of forests or deserts where at no great distance you may find nomade, pastoral communities, with the rudest possible agriculture, and even wild tribes living in a state of nature, with little or no clothing, and subsisting almost exclusively on the natural productions of the forest.

Perhaps the most valuable of all modern improvements in English husbandry are those which, in one way or another, render the farmer less dependent than formerly upon the natural supply of rain; drainage, and in some cases irrigation; various modes of ploughing, planting, manures and machinery, have been discovered by modern agricultural science in England, which enable the farmer of our time to get a crop where his predecessors' crops would have entirely failed, owing to too much or too little rain. In these respects England is far in advance of India.

The Indian farmer, even at the best, is extremely dependent upon the natural supply of the periodical rains; and though much has been done to make up for occasional deficiency by artificial irrigation, what has been hitherto done bears a much less proportion than in England to what remains to be effected, in the way of exempting the agriculturist from the consequences of irregular, deficient, or superabundant rainfall. We shall have occasion to refer again to this fact. It is one of the cardinal points which we have to bear in mind, because it is one of those evils of which the remedy lies in our own power.

2nd cause of English immunity from famine. Power to import foreign grain.

(2.) Another great advantage of the modern English farmer over his brethren in the East is that when his own crops fail, he and his people can buy foreign grain, which reaches them through the aid of good roads and communications, either by land or water. One way and another, the English farmer in the worst of years has something to sell, or has some capital or credit wherewith he can buy the food which the foreign food-producer is able to sell him, and which reaches him at a moderately enhanced price, through a fairly perfect system of sea and land transport and of free commerce.

In all these respects the greater part of the East is infinitely behind Europe. The Bengal labourer especially, with wages at 1½*d.* or 2*d.* a day, and no made roads or canals to bring him food, is always terribly near the brink of starvation. I do not know that there is a single well-ascertained instance of any famine in Asia so extensive, that there were not within what we should, in Europe, call reasonable reach, crops sufficient, if they could have been transported, to have fed the starving, in the adjoining countries. We have historical accounts of famines which desolated half India, and which, at the distance of centuries, are still talked of with horror as traditions of what might possibly recur. But in all these cases there is probability, though there may be no absolute historical proof, that there were, at the same time, good crops within what we should here call very easy reach of the afflicted districts. As regards modern times, however, there can be no doubt that in the worst of famines, within the memory of the last two or three generations, there have always been ample crops which might have fed the starving district, had means of good communication existed. And that will be the case in Bengal, even should our worst anticipations for the present season be fulfilled. There will be good food which might reach the famine-stricken districts if we could carry it. Not always, perhaps, food of the precise kind which the people would naturally prefer; but if they cannot get food, it will be because it cannot be got to them; if they cannot eat it, it will be because some other reason than its want of adaptation to human sustenance prevents its use. We shall recur, farther on, to this part of the subject.

3rd cause. Elaborate social and administrative organisation of England.

(3.) A third great advantage of England and of the greater part of Europe is that the country is well organised, both socially and for administrative purposes. There are not only central and local governments and administrations, but municipal institutions, which are closely connected with the central government, and which place it in intimate and immediate relations with individual families throughout the country by means of parochial or other chains of organisation. There are not only government officials, but the representatives of charitable and religious bodies, and a middle class more or less numerous and well instructed; all of which form a continuous chain between the poorest and the richest, and enable any part of the population which may be straitened for sustenance to receive support from the Government or from richer neighbours.

So far from this being the case in Bengal, there was in that country, till very recently, an absolute and almost impassable gulf between the governors and the governed. The governors were literally a few score of Englishmen, or of persons trained by Englishmen, dispersed at immense intervals over the vast area of Bengal, and confined, partly by law and partly by usage, and by prejudice almost as potent as law, to the collection of revenue from great landlords and to the administration of civil and criminal justice; and, even for this latter purpose, the numbers were so small in comparison to the work to be done, that it was impossible the judicial officers should do their duty thoroughly.

Within my memory the government of the province of Bengal was supposed to be vested in the Governor-General personally, and he had, to assist him in making laws and administering the government of this enormous province, a single Secretary with a few subordinate officers in the secretariat, a Board of Revenue, and two independent Supreme Courts of Justice sitting in Calcutta. So complete was the separation between governors and governed that not even the best informed of the governing classes could tell with any approach to certainty whether the population of the province were 40 or 50 or 60 millions, and though there was of course an immense mass of very valuable recorded information on many subjects, the greater part of Bengal, even within a few days' journey of Calcutta, was much more a terra incognita to the government of India than many of the extreme provinces of its dominion a thousand miles off. This was partly due to the immense area and mass of population to be dealt with, and partly to the ease with which a vast revenue was collected, and any opposition to government put down, but still more to a kind of prejudice, the strength and duration of which forms one of the most curious features in the whole history of our Indian Empire, to trace the origin of which we must go back three quarters of a century.

Bengal "permanent settlement."

After long discussion carried on between Lord Cornwallis and his advisers, who were men of the highest mark as practical statesmen, what was called the "permanent settlement" was introduced into Bengal, the general features of which are too well known to need any description here; according to Lord Cornwallis' ideas this settlement embodied a plan which was to be gradually developed for replacing much of the ancient Indian machinery of internal administration which had been swept away, and for organising local government throughout these provinces. You will find the general features and many of the details of Lord Cornwallis' plans indicated with sufficient clearness in the Bengal Regulations of 1798, and in the Minutes of Lord Cornwallis and his councillors on those enactments. But the author of this great measure left all this supplementary part of his work in embryo. There was nothing to have prevented his work being carried on by his successors, but other pressing wants demanded the attention of succeeding Governors-General, and a superstitious reverence for the permanent settlement grew up, which like other superstitions had no sort of connection with any real respect for the rights created by Lord Cornwallis.

Long after I first went to India it was impossible to

propose any measure of reform in Bengal, however little connected with the principles of Lord Cornwallis' settlement, which might not be, and which not unfrequently was, successfully resisted by the cry that "the permanent settlement was in danger." And to such an extent was this carried, that up to within the last twenty years I do not think there was any part of India in which the district officers knew so little of their districts, and had so little hold upon them, as in this province which ranks among the oldest of our landed possessions in India.

It was not until Lord Dalhousie's time that a separate Lieutenant-Governor was appointed for Bengal. Indirectly, of course, the ruler of Bengal, whether under the name of Secretary to the Governor-General or of Lieutenant-Governor, had enormous power; but his legal and nominal authority is even now more restricted than that of many officers of very inferior grade in provinces not containing a fiftieth part of the population of Bengal, and not paying a hundredth part of what Bengal pays to the State.

Ever since a separate Lieutenant-Governor was first appointed, there has been a steady improvement in the administration of Bengal; one gave Bengal a police, another improved the judicial system, a third fostered education, and so on. But since Sir George Campbell went there, more effectual measures have been taken, than at any former period, to enable the Government to have the same hold over the provinces that it has elsewhere in India; though some of the best devised measures, which have been proposed for this purpose, are still hardly beyond the stage of preliminary discussion. It must take two or three generations of official life before any Viceroy can feel that he has the same kind of grasp of the wants of his subjects and the same power of aiding them within 100 miles of his capital that he possesses over the remotest frontier province of the empire.

It is necessary you should bear this in mind, otherwise Lord Northbrook and Sir George Campbell may be held answerable for the omissions and oversights of their predecessors during the past eighty years; and I can confidently say that no two men have crowded into their terms of office more energetic work intended to supply those omissions, than the present Viceroy and the Lieutenant-Governor of Bengal—though I believe the task is one which would be difficult for half a dozen of the most active of rulers completely to carry out, if their whole lives were devoted to the task.

Want of administrative machinery in Bengal, not general in other parts of India.

It must not be supposed that what I have said of the want of administrative machinery in Bengal applies to every part of India. In many parts an excellent chain of administration from the Viceroy, through a local government, through officers of districts, and village and municipal authorities, places the central government in fair administrative relations with the whole population, and there are many provinces where nothing of importance can take place in any hamlet without its being promptly known throughout the official chain, and, if necessary, communicated to the head of the Government. Sometimes this system is one of our own devising. In the best instances, however, which I know, a good native system has been perfected and perpetuated; but everywhere out of Bengal the facilities for meeting a calamity like the present are far greater than in Bengal itself.

(4.) In drawing a contrast between the condition of England and of India as regards power to resist famine, I must not omit to mention that well-known institution of caste, which is, perhaps, stronger in rural Bengal than in most parts of India. We have nothing at all like the Indian caste in its relations to any questions respecting food, to which I would direct your attention, as giving you any notion of the difficulties which a European administrator will find in feeding the starving population of an Indian province.

4th. Caste.

Even here we have many prejudices with regard to food. We find in our daily life that new articles of food, however excellent in themselves, do not readily make their way among the poor and less instructed classes. They will frequently almost starve rather than eat the best of Australian meat or novel kinds of food; and all who have dealt with the poorest classes in ordinary times, as well as in times of scarcity and famine, know how difficult it is at first to induce parents, who are almost beside themselves for want of food to give to their children, to try the Indian corns, the foreign pulses, and the farinaceous food of various kinds which may frequently be offered them at half the price of wheaten bread or potatoes. But these difficulties, strong as we know them to be among ourselves, are as cobwebs compared to the obstacles interposed by Indian caste.

Remember that, as a general rule, no ordinary Hindoo or Indian Mohammedan may eat food cooked by one, or which has been touched by one, of an inferior caste, nor even drink water from the hands of a man of a lower caste than himself, and that to a very large proportion of the population the meat and the spirituous and fermented liquors, which form so large a proportion of our most nourishing diet, are not only prohibited, but the slightest suspicion of admixture is sufficient to ensure the rejection of the whole tainted mass of the best and most nutritious food. So strong are these prejudices that the greater part of the Indian population, till absolutely beside themselves with the frenzy of hunger, will refuse to eat forbidden food, though it may be of a kind that is considered the most tempting and nutritious by a neighbour of inferior caste. I have known cases of Brahman soldiers, accidentally detained in a transport after their own supply of provisions failed, who quite starved themselves to death without a murmur or word of reproach to any one, rather than subsist on the abundant provisions which were offered them by men of inferior caste in their own corps in the same ship.

There are many means of mitigating these difficulties. Water carriers of a privileged class, and cooks of the highest caste, may be procured, and much of the food which, when first presented, would be declined as novel and therefore unclean, may be so presented with a sort of certificate of orthodoxy as to be thankfully accepted.

But all this involves not only much trouble and arrangement, but great knowledge of the people and infinite patience, and no one whose experience is confined to the poor of other countries can imagine the difficulties of dealing with starving Hindoos, even when you have the most ample means at your disposal.

No natural or inherent incapacity in India, to prevent its being protected from famine as completely as England.

Let us note in passing, that in none of the particulars to which I have alluded is there any natural or inherent superiority of Europe over Asia which can make the European example incapable of imitation in Asia. There are, of course, differences of degree, but there is, as far as my experience goes, no natural or inherent incapacity in Asia which could justify our despairing of being able to protect India as completely against general mortality from famine as we and our ancestors have protected England.

Even as regards caste, it may be cited as an instance of those impediments which are commonly talked of as being insuperable in India, but which are not really incapable of removal. We commonly hear caste talked of as something ancient and immutable; but the researches of modern scholars have shown most clearly that it is by no means ancient—that few of its most antiquated provisions date much farther back than the Norman Conquest, or are as old as some of our own Saxon customs and tenures; some of the caste restrictions are of very modern origin, and the experience of every one who has watched the operations of caste carefully in India, will have shown him that, so far from being immutable, stubborn as it is, and comparatively insensible to influence from without, its laws are nevertheless liable, from a variety of causes, to constant change and modification. Caste is, in fact, a fashion—a fossillized fashion if you will—but still only a fashion, and, like all fashions, subject to a great variety of influences which modify its provisions.*

* I will only give two instances; one of them bearing somewhat on the question before us, as a question of food, the other showing what may be done by a little good sense or perseverance on the part of a single Englishman.

The first occurred many years ago, when potatoes first became a common article of growth in some parts of India. It was speedily found that they were very well adapted to some soils and climates in India, that there was a constant market for them among the English, and that they were a very excellent article of food for all mankind; but it was beyond all question that they were introduced by the unclean

Partially connected with caste there are two points of essential difference between India and England which must not go unnoticed.

---

foreigners, and there were not wanting among the more bigoted Brahmans some who asserted that they clearly partook of the nature of flesh, inasmuch as they could never be grown without animal manure; that they were like all other flesh food, unclean; and that their introduction was simply one of the many devices of the foreigner to interfere with the caste of the Hindoos. By some agency, which I have never been able to trace, the question was at length referred to a Brahmanical Council of learned Shastris at Benares. The questions at issue were debated at great length, and a decision was arrived at, not only affirming that potatoes were clearly vegetable, but that they belonged to a class of vegetable food which might be lawfully eaten by the most rigid Brahman on days when grain food of every kind was strictly prohibited. Since the promulgation of this decree of the Brahmanical Council, potatoes have entered largely into the food of the better class of Hindoos in many parts of the country, and their cultivation is constantly extending.

The other instance may sound ridiculous, but it would not have been so had caste carried the day. In Western India the usual dress of a respectable class of natives analogous to that from which our railway porters are drawn in this country, is a pair of cotton trousers, and a cotton coat varying in length from a jacket to a surtout. When the first section of the Great Indian Peninsula Railway, the first railway which was opened in India, was completed, one of the English railway officials engaged a body of the best men he could procure as railway porters, and they were to be presented with new dresses, uniform in colour and make; but, when the dresses were finished, and paraded on the persons of the future porters, the practised eye of the Englishman immediately observed that the flowing skirts, which had been made with unusual liberality, were absolutely incompatible with safety and efficiency, as they might catch against handles or projections of carriages, or impede the activity of the wearer. He therefore gave an order that when on duty the coat tails should always be tucked in under the trousers—an arrangement which, though it had many practical advantages, was obviously unpicturesque and unusual. The order was received in silence, and for the moment obeyed; but directly

Advantage of English labourer in quantity and variety of food.

One will have already occurred to you in the variety of food which is, or can be, used by even the lowest class of Englishmen. Poorly fed, as many of our very poor still are in England, they are all, as a class, capable of subsisting, in times of need, on something less than their usual allowance in ordinary times, and, however prejudiced they are, all are ready on pressing occasions to accept a change in their usual diet.

So far from this being the case in India, though I believe the existing population of India is, as a mass, better fed than it was forty years ago, still there are large masses, especially in Bengal, living on the limits of starvation, and who, although half-starved, are, by usage and prejudice, restricted to one kind of food, and that not the most nutritious—I mean an inferior kind of rice. Hence a degree of scarcity and consequent dearness which would starve thousands in India would only slightly straiten the poorest classes in this country. You will remember that this difficulty was very clearly brought out in the case

---

the Englishman's back was turned, a caste meeting was held, for most of the new porters were of one caste, and it was unanimously resolved that the tucking in the skirts of their coats was contrary to usage, and to the rules of their caste, and that they would strike in a body. As the railway was to open immediately, the mutineers thought they had the "Sahib" on the hip, and that he must comply at least in the first instance; but they were no match for the resources and determination of the Englishman. He required them to divest themselves at once of the garments in dispute, summoned the whole body of station sweepers, who were of an infinitely lower caste, and announced his determination of at once promoting them one and all to the position of porters and to the possession of the new garments, unless his orders were instantly complied with. Immediate obedience was the result; the skirts were tucked in; and from that day there was no mutiny of the kind while that Superintendent ruled.

of the classes who usually subsisted on potatoes in Ireland; and here again the Irish difficulty is identical with the Indian difficulty, only that the latter is greatly magnified.

Another feature connected with caste, which must not be forgotten, is the power which the poorest in England have to change their occupation when that which is usual to them does not afford them a subsistence. We have, it is true, daily examples of the difficulty of any such change in this country. In the east of London, when the ship-building trade is slack; in Lancashire, when the cotton manufacture is restricted; in the agricultural districts, when the population is in excess of the demand for field labourers, some of our best and most intelligent men in the lower classes find it not easy at once to change their occupation; but what is only a difficulty in England is rendered almost impossible in India, owing to the iron restrictions of caste, which render a man liable to every social disqualification should he change the occupation of his forefathers. I have said "almost" impossible because even in India the power of caste in this respect is not absolute, and is daily decreasing, though generations must elapse before it becomes as easy for an Indian labourer to choose his particular form of labour as it is in Europe.

And in power to vary the form of his labour.

Before quitting the subject of the causes of famines, I would say a few words with reference to the cause which has been assigned, but I believe erroneously, as one of those leading to a want of food. I allude to the largely-increased growth of other products than food over a great area of Bengal. It has been said that the cultivation of articles such as opium, cotton, silk, sugar, but, above all, jute in Bengal is one cause of a diminished production of grain and of

Growth of exportable produce *not* a cause of deficient supplies of food.

consequent want of food. I do not think that this cause will stand examination. There can be no doubt in the mind of anyone who knows the cultivators of India, that they are neither so blind to their own interests nor so wedded to old practices as to grow any crops other than those which they believe will pay them best, and they are at least as sagacious as English farmers in choosing what crops they will grow, so far as their powers and knowledge go. It will invariably be found that they never make up their mind to sow any crop but grain, unless they think, according to the latest received intelligence, that some other crop will pay them better; and anyone may satisfy himself, by a very short inquiry, that every variation in the Colonial Produce Market in England or New York is now followed by an immediate expansion or contraction of the growth of that produce in India, if it happens to be one of the Indian staples. Such produce is in many ways more advantageous to the grower than grain. His surplus grain is difficult to sell except to his own village dealer and money-lender; but exportable produce will always command a cash price at the nearest market town, and this cash price will invariably be found to be greatly in excess of what, according to his calculations when he sowed it, the farmer could afford to pay for imported grain. Of course his calculations may be deranged by unexpected changes in the markets or the season, but the same might occur in Yorkshire.

At any rate, it is quite clear that, even if the cause in question were a true one, which I believe it is not, nothing that Government or private benevolence could do could possibly supply a remedy. No one in his senses would dream of a Government prohibition to grow cotton or jute, nor of a benevolent zemindar growing grain habitually, when jute would pay him better, merely because he believed that by growing jute he might diminish the aggregate supply of food. It is quite clear that if in these matters we let the farmers alone to grow what they find pays them best, it is the fault of the Government in not giving roads and means of communication, if they are not always able to buy a sufficiency of grain from other quarters to feed the labourers on the land devoted to jute or other exportable produce.

III.

Present measures which may be taken to mitigate the evils of famine.

We now come to the important question: What is it possible for the Government of India to do at the present moment, with a view to avert or mitigate the worst evils of the threatened scarcity of food?

And, first, I must remind you of what the Government of India really consists. Here in England you have the Secretary of State, the representative of the really governing authority of all India, the Government and Parliament of Imperial England. He is aided with advisers, who are supposed to represent much accumulated experience of official life in India; but you must not think that any part of the Government in England has anything to say to the *initiation* of measures necessary to meet a famine in India.

The Government here may, of course, suggest, as may the press or any private individual, and after the result approve or disapprove the measures taken, and the Government here may—and I need not assure you will—send out everything the authorities in India may find they need in the shape of men, material, or money for such a contest as the Government of India has to sustain; but no previous sanction on the part of the Government at home is necessary to enable the Viceroy to meet a calamity like that which we fear impends over Bengal. The Government of India and the local government of Bengal are all powerful, as far as any existing official machinery can be powerful, to do what is immediately needed; and I will presently describe the sort of measures which I have no doubt will be taken in due time, to do all that human agency can do, as rulers towards ruled, to mitigate the inevitable consequences of a wide-spread scarcity of food. I say this, not to avert by anticipation any possible censure of the home authorities, but to prevent confusion, and to do justice. All that can here be done is to appoint the best men, and to support them manfully in such difficulties as lie before them. They will need all the support we here at home can give them, and to them will justly belong the whole credit of success. But I speak from experience when I say that in such cases, after the danger has been once realised, and full authority given with every assurance of hearty and energetic support and sympathy, it is not easy for those at a distance to guide wisely, or to prevent advice from becoming embarrassing.

I need not tell you that in those who now fill the offices of Viceroy and of Lieut.-Governor of Bengal will be found every quality which could give Englishmen confidence that this great trust will be worthily discharged. It may seem presumptuous in me to say so, but I cannot help stating my own conviction that it would be difficult to find, in the whole range of English statesmen and administrators, men more capable of rising to a worthy discharge of the Herculean task before them.

The first thing, of course, to be done is to realise the danger, and regarding this I think there can be no kind of doubt. Whether the most sanguine or the gloomiest views of what is coming should be justified by the result, this much at least is certain—that on no previous occasion has the attention of the Government of India or of the local government been so early directed to impending scarcity as during the present year. I know that before the first note of alarm was sounded, as it always must be on these occasions, through the public press, great anxiety had been felt by some of the highest officials in Bengal regarding the prospects of the season. You must remember that a good or bad season depends often on the rainfall within a single fortnight, and that the well-grounded fears of the more intelligent Bengal planters and zemindars are necessarily communicated at as early a date to the English public through a telegram in your morning newspapers, as they can be to the Indian Viceroy at Simla.

Danger must be realised.

Then, the danger having been adequately realised, and being, on the most favourable calculation, a national evil of gigantic proportions, it only remains that the Government should at once, to use an expression which I have seen quoted, "declare war upon the famine;" and this has been already done in the most unmistakable form. There is not a government official from one end of Bengal to the other who is not at this moment fully aware that he will be required, by rulers the most intelligent and most exacting, to strain every nerve and every faculty of his being, to prevent the death from starvation of the Queen's subjects.

"War must be declared" on the famine.

It is, of course, all important to know as early as possible what will require to be done, and here we are met in Bengal with the difficulties created by the absence of administrative machinery, on which I have already dealt, and which prevents us from having accurate statistics of the probable wants of any district.

Want of accurate statistics.

We are not well off here in England for agricultural statistics; but the want is supplied by a thousand channels of private information, which enable us during any crisis to supply in some measure the defect of accurate official statistics. But in Bengal even Sir George Campbell, who is one of the best informed men on every subject of the kind in India, will find himself sadly in want of any but the vaguest and most general particulars as to the probable extent of the scarcity.

No question is more frequently asked than what Government estimate can be given of the probable extent of the famine and the probable extent of the demand for food grain which will be required during the coming year; and I have heard great surprise expressed that Government is not in possession of accurate particulars in both respects. Therefore let me remind you that the immediate cause of the famine—the failure of the usual autumn rains—could not have excited alarm till October, and that famine could not have been well foreseen till some weeks later; and that, though we are bound now to prepare for the worst, it is still possible the famine may be mitigated through the winter rains.

Let me also remind you that in no famine of which we have any experience in this country, say, for instance, the Irish famine, was it found possible to make accurate estimates beforehand, or till a period so late in the duration of the famine, that almost every useful hand under Government was employed at the utmost stretch of his powers in meeting the immediate wants of emergency. In fact, it was not till after the worst of the famine was over that accurate statistics of what had been its extent, and what had been the amount of food which would have kept the people alive, could be prepared. Now, this was the case in Ireland, where, probably, the agricultural statistics are better than in any part of the United Kingdom; and you may, therefore, be able to judge of the difficulty of any accurate calculation or prediction regarding Bengal, where the agricultural statistics are certainly the loosest and most imperfect in all India, and probably throughout the whole of the British Empire.

But there are some large facts which may at once give us some useful guess regarding the points referred to, and at the same time may show that this is not a case in which we can fairly find fault with officers on the spot because they cannot give more accurate data. It is clearly shown in all the evidence which is as yet accessible, that an area containing a population more than five times as great as that of Ireland, is threatened with an almost total failure of one of the largest food crops on which the people usually subsist. It is also clear that, in every point of comparison between Ireland and India, the comparison is unfavourable to India in a direction which greatly increases all the difficulties of the administration in time of scarcity; and, therefore, it may safely be said that the calamity which threatens us is at least five times as great as that which occurred in Ireland, and that the Government of India will be indeed fortunate if it has not upon its hands five times as many mouths to feed as were at any time to be fed by the Government in Ireland.*

* The following extracts from the *Friend of India*, of Nov. 21st, and the *Times of India*, of Nov. 24th, 1873, give a recent Indian estimate of the probable extent of the evil :— [Regarding

Fortunately there are circumstances in Bengal which render it possible for a man with great resources of

---

Regarding the approaching famine the *Friend of India* says:—

"In a circular dated the 17th instant, and sent to all commissioners and district officers in Bengal, very full and detailed instructions are given regarding the scarcity and famine. The replies to the circular of 13th October show that, roughly speaking, extreme failure of crops will probably be confined to all the Patna Division, all the Bhagulpore Division except the Sonthal country, and to the districts of Dinagepore, Rungpore, and Bograh, and parts of Rajshaye, Maldah, and Moorshedabad, in the Rajshaye Division. In other districts there will be short crops, but in the districts and parts of districts above named the whole yield of all the food-crops of 1873-74 will, unless copious rain falls at a very early date, probably be below a six-anna crop all round; and relief works on a more or less extended scale will be required soon. There are other districts or parts of districts where the crop has been short, and where relief works may be required a little later if not now, such for instance as the Maunbhoom district, much of the Burdwan Division, and some limited portions of the Presidency Division. But in all these districts the harvests all round are expected to give an eight-anna crop; and though food will be dear, there will, it may be hoped, be no general and complete failure of the food supply. For the present, then, and for the purposes of these orders, the tracts named in the first part of this paragraph will be treated as the distressed districts. At the same time the Commissioners of Burdwan and Chota Nagpore should watch narrowly whether large portions of the Burdwan Division and the Maunbhoom district may require to be brought within this category. Some relief measures will no doubt be necessary in these tracts, where there is a large labouring population, many of whom may be without employment as soon as the rice harvest is over.

"Government will look to the natural operations of trade to import the food required to fill the deficit in the local supply in the districts where the crop has failed. By way of facilitating this traffic, the Government has reduced by one-half the railway grain rates, and has also ordered the temporary abolition of all road toll-bars, or tolls on ferries which can in dry weather be crossed by a ford or a causeway. The tolls on ferries where boats must be used to ferry carts across are to be reduced to the lowest tariff that will remunerate the boatmen. Further, the Government has put a steamer and flats to ply on the

money, and authority at his command and disposal, with a steady determination to use them to the utmost, to do

---

Ganges from Kooshteah to Rajshaye, and has ordered a small light-draught steamer with flats to ply on the inland waters of Rajshaye. All that local officers have to do is to see that neither at ferries, nor at railway stations, nor at ghats, nor on rivers, are any unauthorized difficulties placed in the way of, or dues levied upon, the transport of grain, and that the roads are put in order, and every facility given for traffic.

"In places likely to be in want, where there may not be traders of sufficient means and in sufficient numbers to import food to fill the deficit in the food supplies, or where for any reason the natural flow of trade is slow and difficult, the Government is ready to aid and promote the natural trade of the country by making advances of money, either—

(*a*) To zemindars, planters, or others, on condition that they will import grain from a distance and sell it as near as possible at cost price, all expenses included.

(*b*) To traders and others of a safe and responsible character, who will take the money at a moderate interest of 6 per cent. per annum, and will engage to import grain from a distance without any conditions as to the rate or manner of their selling it.

"The Lieutenant-Governor delegates to district officers in the distressed districts the power of making such advances, where necessary, up to a limit of Rs. 2000 to any person; and to Commissioners in those districts the power of sanctioning advances up to a limit of Rs. 10,000 to any one person. Larger advances may be specially sanctioned, or a larger discretion may be allowed on a representation of the circumstances. In the former class of advances an undertaking must be taken from the person receiving the advance that he will repay the advance without interest before the 31st December, 1874, or will produce full and complete accounts to show why Government should forego any portion of the payment. In the latter class of advances it will be necessary merely to stipulate that the supplies will be drawn from districts beyond those to which the scarcity extends, and for repayment of the principal and interest by the end of 1874 or any earlier date that may be arranged. It will also be desirable to stipulate for the occasional inspection of the grain invoices (chalans) of such dealers in order to verify that they really do import their grain from a distance.

more than any Englishman, who does not know what his countrymen can do when they are put to it, would be inclined to believe possible.

"The Lieutenant-Governor has full confidence that district officers will know what persons can be trusted to act fairly by Government and by the people in respect of advances of these kinds. In regard to all advances for grain, the Lieutenant-Governor thinks it essential that it should be a distinct stipulation that the purchases should be made and the grain imported at a very early date to be specified, so that the means of carriage now existing may be utilised to the utmost. If the purchasers are allowed to delay, and the despatches do not come till February or March, all the difficulty which the Lieutenant-Governor apprehends from a block of carriage will probably arise and the advances will do very little good.

"The works sanctioned for the class who labour for wages are then again stated. In the rest of the circular local officers are desired to push on the preparation of relief works in as many parts as possible of the distressed districts. Statements of extra establishments required for, and probable expenditure on relief works, are asked for from Commissioners. The views of Government as to storage of grain and its sale at relief works are stated. Officers are directed at once to select sites, and to prepare storage for reception of Government grain. Report is called for regarding the means of transport in the district and its improvement. The need for early testing of transporting agency is enjoined. Officers are directed to prepare plans of arrangements, and machinery for relief committees and relief centres, and to report through the Commissioner. Loans to municipalities, and landholders and others for permanent improvements are to be promoted, and the terms on which these loans are obtainable should be made known to the people. Grants are made to each division to cover their advances. A weekly narrative is to be sent direct from Government from each distressed district, every Monday. Authority is given to Commissioners to sanction works, and to authorize, temporarily, establishments for grain storage, transport, and relief works, within certain limits, and subject to weekly report. When Relief Committees are established the Government will at once make to every committee a grant equal to the amount of its private subscriptions, and may, when distress goes very far, be still more liberal. If a relief committee requires grain for its relief houses, before it can import for itself, the Magistrate will have authority

Having made the best estimate in his power as to where food will be required and in what quantities, the

---

to advance all the grain he can spare from the Government stores collected for labourers on relief works. In regard to the promotion of emigration to the tea districts, or to other parts of the country where population may be sparse, the Lieutenant-Governor will issue instructions hereafter.

"The District Reports for the week ending Saturday continue to deepen in gloom. These may be taken as types." . . . .

And then follow long details of "rice crop lost beyond hope," "land dried up, and unfit for second sowing," "prospects of cold weather crops very small," &c., &c. But these may, of course, be modified by cold weather rainfall.

The *Times of India* adds: "The area of the drought and apprehended scarcity in Bengal, thanks to foresight, promptitude, and method in collecting and recording current information, is not only accurately known to the authorities of that presidency, but is tolerably well understood all over India. But let us, for convenience' sake, just sketch in outline the geography of the districts over which, in metaphor, we say the dark cloud of famine impends; though, in fact, it is there the heavens are brass and the earth iron, while the pitiless sun shines with a fierceness unmitigated even by the usual slight moisture of the Bengal atmosphere. The now rainless tract lies chiefly far north of the Ganges, though it spreads down to the great river, even to Patna, where the affluent Gunduk may be said to mark the western boundary of the parched territory, which then stretches, with more or less regularity, nearly across to the Bramahputra, coming down between the two rivers so as to enclose Malda and the once semi-regal district of Moorshedabad. Even on the east of the last-named large river at Dacca and Mymensing, just within the area of 75 inches rainfall, the fields have refused their usual yield. We must not forget, also, that the extreme south-west of the now arid stretch of country reaches across to the right bank of the great river extending from Baugulpore to Patna, and reaching far back into the Sonthal hill districts of uncomfortable memory. This is sufficiently full a delineation for readers in this part of India to bear well in mind; and the only further definition we need make a note of is that the western portion of the famine tract is the driest in all years—though it is all within an average annual rainfall of 50 or 60 inches—and will now suffer more severely than the

first step of course is to secure such an amount of food as Government is likely to need to feed those who in the

---

rest week after week. As special public works are undertaken, tolls are suspended, and remissions of land revenue granted, we shall all gradually acquire a fuller knowledge of the topography of northern, western, and central Bengal than we should otherwise have cared to acquire.

"After all the pains taken in the great census of Bengal, the results of which are set forth with so much discretion and skill in Mr. Beverley's big report, it is rather disappointing to notice that the records are not complete in that portion of social statistics with which it is specially important the authorities of that presidency should, at this crisis, be fully acquainted." The writer then shows at length the absence of any reliable statistics as to the numbers of any agricultural or other "labourers," and proceeds:—"The chief practical question for those on whom rests the responsibility for saving these million souls alive is, how many mouths will require to be fed? After all, the writer whom we have referred to can only give a two-fold reply, one portion of which is suspiciously distinct—namely, that the destitute 'residuum' will amount to one-tenth of the whole population of the drought-stricken districts, that is, about 2,250,000 people, small and great—and the other is uncomfortably vague, namely, that 'ryots who farm even a very little land will be able to get on somehow.' This latter supposition would, we hope, hold good over most of Western India if placed under similar adverse circumstances, seeing that our ryots always retain some portion of proprietary right, and—except where the new settlements have cut 'into the quick'—some little agricultural stock and household stuff. Probably in the north-west provinces, also, it might prove partially true, where, notwithstanding the pro-landlord superstition, under cover of which something approaching to a rack-rent is paid by the cultivator, the fertility of the soil is such as always to leave fruit, vegetables, or roots within the peasant's reach. But what can be said about the cultivating ryots over the Behar border being able to 'get on somehow'? If we look at the dark-brown patch covering Sarun, Patna, and Tirhoot, on the Census map, which indicates a density of population from 690 to 778 per square mile, and remember that the peasantry, under the operation of a grinding landlord system, have, in these districts, been crushed down into the chronic destitution of abject serfs, we shall see how little hope there

long run will be thrown helplessly upon its hands, and who unless fed by Government or by private charity, must starve.

---

is for four or five million of souls in those three provinces 'getting on' at all. No doubt the promise of the Empire, given and now being fulfilled by the Viceroy and the Lieut.-Governor of Bengal, will avail against the terrible odds which hunger has on its side in Northern Behar; but the thoughtful administrator will consider that there must be something abnormal in the constitution and conditions of a society which requires such extraordinary efforts to keep it from being all but swept away. The executive officers of Bengal have been thoroughly aroused to meet the exigency that has arisen; and without stopping to criticise the somewhat windy resolution first issued, we may feel tolerably confident that, as the peril has been confronted in time, there will be good sense and discretion shown in all the measures that may be taken to meet the emergency. But for us, looking on from a distance, it is permitted to raise the question, as we have just now incidentally, how can these things be? How is it that in these territories of amazing fertility the wages of a labourer for hire are spoken of as having 'risen,' seeing that they have reached 'even threepence' per day, and that, 'in some districts, day labourers may even earn as much as sixpence per day at busy seasons'?

"The notion of over-population, which is a symptom as much as a cause, will not suffice to account for the flagrant contrast, presented in these fertile districts, between the gifts of God and the condition of His creatures. Although compared with its natural resources and capabilities, Behar is far poorer than is supposed in Europe, there is undoubtedly a large amount of wealth raised in the province, a considerable amount of which is expended in barren litigation by the zemindars and other superior landholders. Undoubtedly there is a sufficient surplus amount of production to afford a year's subsistence in advance for the whole population. Why then is it that we find the masses of the population not only without even six months' stock in hand, but a large portion of them who very shortly will be entirely destitute of daily food? No doubt a dozen causes might be cited as contributing towards this unnatural state of things; but it seems to us the one inclusive and over-mastering cause of this ghastly impoverishment of the peasantry in Bengal and Behar is indicated with sufficient distinctness on pp. 43–4, of the 'Bengal Administration Report for 1871–2.' The

It is easy to see that in a case like this, great measures are absolutely necessary, but it is equally evident that the great measures must not be of a kind to increase the dreaded evil. For instance, if we sweep into the Government stores the stores of a corn dealer, which, if left in his hands, would be carefully doled out to persons able and willing to pay for food, we clearly do worse than if we did nothing; it is impossible we can feed these people as punctually or as economically as they themselves and the grain dealer would feed them. I do not mean economy of money, for that must be left entirely out of our calcula-

---

writer after showing that 'the early Regulations (of 1793-1802) were most careful in their provisions for restraining the zemindars and protecting the ryots,' goes on to point out that while there has in modern times 'been a general tendency much to insist upon, and indeed exaggerate the rights and privileges conferred on the landlord by the permanent settlement, there has been at the same time an equal disposition to forget, evade, and ignore the terms, conditions, and obligations attached to those rights and privileges by the very Regulations which conferred or confirmed them.'

"We need not pursue this formidable and painful topic here; but the civilians and journalists of Bengal trained in association with this hateful landed system and rendered callous by familiarity, cannot be expected to perceive the full deformity of the social organisation around them. Hence it is more incumbent on observers at a distance to do what they can to make the terrible lessons of the next few months sink into the minds of those who can deduce from them true guidance for the future. There is another general consideration that applies to these famine districts to which we should draw attention, namely, the almost total absence of artificial irrigation in the district now suffering from drought. Rivers they have, but the great P.W.D. has not yet shown the people how to utilise them. The Soane Irrigation Works, of which we hear so much, as the grand relief works, are all south of the Ganges. Will no strong engineer rise superior to the routine of the department, and show how the people can be employed north of the Ganges in promoting a general effort to secure tank, well, and small canal irrigation from the Gunduk, the Kusi, and the (*chota*) Mahanudi?" [*Vide* also Appendix A.]

tion in this part of the business, but economy of grain. We should be taking the grain from careful distributors and careful consumers, and render them dependent upon the necessarily lavish management of a Government dépôt.

Let us then lay down as the first rule to be observed by Government that it shall provide stores of its own without stint, to the utmost limits of any possible demand, without, if possible, doing anything which shall add to the embarrassment of those whose natural and usual function it is to preserve and distribute the grain supplies of the country. Hence Government may properly buy and store up grain which is likely to be exported, and by coming forward as a great purchaser of imported grain, or by offering bounties on import, may usefully stimulate the inflow of grain from without.

Storage of grain.

It has been suggested that Government should prohibit the export of grain from India, and we hear of differences of opinion on this subject between the highest officials in India. The Governor-General is said to be opposed to any prohibition of the kind, and I feel sure he is right, for many reasons.

Prohibition of exports to be avoided.

First, the prohibition would be ineffectual. If it will pay to export grain, the grain will surely be exported, either through French ports or by other means, which would enable the foreign consumer to outbid the Indian.

The only effectual prohibition of export will be a rise in prices in India; and this can only be delayed by any official prohibition of export. It will be delayed by numerous causes which a moment's reflection will suggest to you, and which need not be here detailed.

But worse than this, any prohibition of export must at once intensify the evil. Local prohibitions of export, or discouragements where there is no power of prohibition, are among the favourite native methods of meeting a scarcity. Like many other such expedients they are selfish and short-sighted, and like everything selfish and short-sighted, they are bad policy.

Throughout India and round the borders are numerous states more or less independent, which would not be slow to follow the Governor-General's example, if he once were to sanction a prohibition of export from India. They always do so when they get alarmed.

When a famine in Rajpootana, only two or three years ago, carried off its hundreds of thousands, most of the little Rajpootana States, instead of making roads and encouraging imports, prohibited the export of grain from their own dominions; and those who did so lost by thousands not only their own but their neighbours' subjects, who might have been their customers, and thus have saved their lives.

During the whole of the recent Persian famine, one of the worst that has been known of late years in Asia (whether we look to the imbecility of the Government or of the people), the exportation of grain was strictly prohibited; and though, as I have said, such prohibitions were very ineffectual, they were sufficiently potent entirely to derange trade, and to prevent import when import was possible.

Now Lord Northbrook's determination not to prohibit export leaves him free to use all the immense influence at his command to prevent resort to the same measure by those who would adopt it even without his suggestion.

He can now reasonably say to every native potentate that abstinence from this suicidal measure will be a mark of loyalty to the British Government, and of effectual desire on the part of the ruler to bear a part in sustaining the burthens of the English rule in the East.

But supposing the Viceroy to give way and to prohibit export, what could he possibly say to the King of Burmah or Siam, nay to the Nizam or the Ruler of Nepaul, or to any of the thousand feudatories who in measures of this kind manage their own affairs, under their own local authority, if he found that they were adopting in their own little way the same measure which he had adopted for the whole of India? It would be something worse than illogical to forbid any little Hill Rajah to impound the few hundredweights of grain which his merchants might otherwise carry down to the Plains of Bengal.

I have said I would not mention expense in this branch of the subject. We are "at war with famine," and in war requisitions of course are not only permissible but necessary. But no sensible civilised general, when he makes a requisition from persons whose aid he may again require, fails either to pay for what he wants, or at least to promise payment from the vanquished party. Now, in this case, prohibition of export differs in nothing but degree from confiscation of stocks; and though, no doubt, such confiscation may, under certain circumstances, be justifiable, it is not, I submit, a wise measure with which to begin the campaign, when you know that your wants further on will far outreach the possible means of supply, unless you carry with you the entire goodwill of the supplying community.

There are large communities of Bengalees out of Bengal, at Ceylon, at Mauritius, and in the West Indies, who habitually feed upon Bengal rice, and for whom more especially the usual exports of Bengal are destined. These people will, of course, be unable to see why they should be starved or straitened to feed their less enterprising brethren who have remained at home. And

I may mention, as a matter of fact, that the most urgent representations have been already received from persons interested in all these colonies, pointing out the disastrous effects which must be produced were the Viceroy to prohibit the exportation of rice—a prohibition, the removal of which would necessarily depend entirely on the view which might be taken of the necessities of the case by the officials on the spot.

It is not likely that merchants at a distance would feel any great confidence in the commercial judgment of the officials to whose power their cargoes would have to be thus consigned, and a general distrust, and holding back in distant grain markets, would be the inevitable result.

If Bengal could have been entirely fed by grain grown in Bengal, something might be said in favour of a prohibition of export. But we all know that sufficient grain does not exist, and that if export be interfered with, except in the way of raising prices by purchase, import will necessarily be discouraged.

If the famine should assume the proportions we apprehend, the whole amount of food which Bengal will require to draw from other sources than its own soil will be so large, that the whole of the exportable quantity furnished by even an average year, could it be at once impounded, would be but a drop in the ocean. Every country from which grain can be brought by telegraph and steam within the next four months must be laid under contribution, and it would be impossible to devise a more effectual mode of paralysing the energies of all who could contribute to this supply, than by letting it go forth that Government was prohibiting the export of grain from Bengal, or in any way interfering with its movement, except by giving every facility to its transport.

I see that some of the advocates for prohibition of export confound such a measure with the *prevention of export by purchasing*, on account of Government, the grain which would be otherwise exported. I need not tell you that no things can be more entirely and essentially distinct in their character and operation than the two measures. Every pound of grain now lying for export at Calcutta and bought up by Government must encourage imports, but every such pound arbitrarily prevented by order of Government from being exported must tend in more ways than one to discourage imports. The one is a measure stimulating natural operations of trade, the other is a measure thwarting and tending to paralyze those natural operations. The one is as wise a step as can be taken under the circumstances, the other, in my opinion, one of the most unwise. But you will at once see that the two measures have nothing whatever in common.

Nor is there any connection between the Viceroy's determination not to prohibit exports, and a blind and inert "trust in the *ordinary supplies of trade.*" The Government may, and no doubt will, purchase and import largely on its own account. This will be an artificial and temporary addition to the ordinary *supplies* of trade; but it will be all in the ordinary *course* of commerce. An additional and powerful purchaser will come into the market; but such a purchaser will not interfere with the *ordinary course of trade.* He will simply stimulate its operations, and his purchases, if wisely and judiciously made, as we may feel confident they will be, can only have the effect of stimulating import from afar, and so of supplying deficiency of local production.*

* *Vide* Appendix D.

IV.

Maintenance of existing social and administrative organisation.

To meet even a moderate scarcity and very partial famine, it will be above all things necessary to keep up and strengthen such administrative organisation as already exists, and to prevent the people crowding in a helpless herd to die of disease, or starve at places remote from their own homes. Though the government administrative organisation in Bengal is, as I have said, singularly weak and in every way inefficient, the necessities of the people have always maintained a quasi municipal organisation of their own, the existence of which is often very little suspected by government officials.

One of the earliest tasks towards meeting the famine will be to trace out and develop such organisation as exists, whether official or unofficial, and to prepare to strengthen and use it towards managing the people, and keeping, as far as possible, in their own homes those who are not likely to live elsewhere. The most healthy state of things would be, of course, that all who can earn wages at a distance, should go to a distance and earn food for themselves, and, if possible, for their families. The little strength the very young, and the very old, and the very worst nourished possess, should not be expended in fruitless journeying, but they should be kept near their own homes, where, if food can be brought to them, a much smaller supply will suffice to keep them alive than could possibly sustain them if they travelled away in vague search of employment. It will be difficult to effect this, but, as I shall show farther on, not impossible, even in India.

V.

The great task of all will be, not only to provide the food, but to transport and distribute it. Let us suppose that Government has wisely calculated the number of mouths it will have to feed, without adding to them any that can possibly be fed by their own exertions. Let us suppose that the millions of tons of food necessary for this purpose are secured at some of the great commercial centres in Bengal; how is this food to be conveyed and distributed over famine-stricken districts which, at the smallest present computation, are five times as large as were the famine-stricken districts of Ireland. Sir George Balfour, in one of his excellent letters published in the "*Times*" has pointed out the great amount of carriage required in a roadless country where the surface of the ground becomes impassable to laden vehicles as soon as a few showers of rain fall, and where, without rain, there is no forage for the draught-cattle. He has shown the consequent inutility of large stores, if they are too many miles from the mouths to be fed; and the necessity for making the most of the dry season to effect the distribution of grain. The task is, in truth, a gigantic one. I am certain it will be faced with a determination to achieve it; but let us here consider for a moment some of the measures which will doubtless be adopted.

Transport of food.

Note first of all, that there is no time to be lost. The telegraph tells us that the labourers of the famine-stricken district are already crowding wherever they hear of work. They will not beg for food while they can earn it. Many of the able-bodied population are already moving in search of work and of food. Evidently, then, one of the first things to be done is to provide as much work as possible.

We all know the usually improvident character of what are called "Famine Works"—works undertaken to provide employment, not works undertaken because they were previously known to be necessary and likely to be executed; but it is one of the consequences of the undeveloped state of Bengal, that in no part of the country is there any lack of work which might at once be undertaken, if the Government had any means to mark it out, to set the task and pay for it.

Famine relief works.

Throughout some of the districts where the crops have failed worst, run the lines of some of the great canals and railway works, and works of drainage, which, from time to time, have been devised by former governments, and which only await an easier state of the finances to be undertaken in any year. Doubtless the Government will call forth from its records all such plans as are in a state to admit of early execution. It will summon to its aid, from every part of India, all available officers, civil or military, and will at once commence as much of the digging and embanking as can be laid out, and will thus provide for the able-bodied not only food, but something with which they can possibly feed their families at a distance.*

* It would be possible to dilate to almost any extent on works which might be undertaken in Bengal to afford employment within reach of some at least of the able-bodied poor who will be reduced to starvation by the famine; but the following are a few of the schemes of irrigation and communication which are said to be in a state to be started at once, as well-considered remunerative works, such as will not only afford work now, but may help to save crops and life in all time to come.

1st. The Soane Canal, projected by Col. Dickens, and now in progress, for the irrigation of districts south of the Ganges, near where the prospect of famine is worst. One of the canals which will extend from Monghyr to Mirzapoor, will, it is said, be 180 feet wide at bottom, with a full supply depth of 8 feet. The total length will be about 180 miles,

But works of this kind are, after all, necessarily scores of miles apart, and require much superintendence to pre-

---

of which 30 miles only have yet been excavated to half the full section. On this part, of course, there will be much room for additional excavation work at once. The whole work is of immense importance to irrigation, and still more as forming the connecting link between the Lower Ganges and the Great Ganges Canal in the north-western provinces. It is admirably adapted for a relief work, as large numbers could be massed on it; and it will not be very far from the railway, so that food supplies for the labourers can be thrown in at many different points along the line. All this has been anticipated by Lord Northbrook, and the Lieutenant-Governor refers in his reports to the excellent effect of the additional work already sanctioned on the Main Trunk Canal. There are other smaller branch canals, which are still very large works, each 40 to 50 miles in length, which form parts of the Soane scheme, and it is believed from the latest advices that some of these have been put in hand, and more, probably, will be undertaken as the necessity arises.

2ndly. There are two great schemes on the Gunduk, north of the Ganges, between the Chumparan and Tirhoot districts on the one side, and Sahran on the other, through the middle of one great region of distress. One at least of these may probably be started at once; and this, we may be sure, will not be lost sight of by the local authorities, by the irrigation officers, and the other advisers of Government.

3rdly. There is the Damooda Canal, a project brought forward by Col. Rundall in Lord Mayo's time, the head works of which were said to have been actually begun, but since suspended. This great work will no doubt be resumed. It is said that some of the works have been sanctioned on a very reduced scale, but the entire great work has been deliberately approved, and was only suspended on account of immediate want of funds. Its resumption, therefore, at the present moment in its integrity, as a means of giving work, will not only remove immediate distress, but be ultimately of immense future benefit to the country.

These three schemes were calculated to afford irrigation for at least 2,500,000 acres. It is needless to remark what would be the value of irrigation works of this magnitude, not dependent on the vicissitudes of season.

4thly. But the great work of all for irrigation, as well as navigation, in Bengal would be Sir Arthur Cotton's proposed canal, leading off from

vent their doing more harm, in causing crowding and consequent disease, than good in relieving famine; and in every part of Bengal, probably, there is work of some

---

the Ganges near Rajmahal, and joining the tide-waters near Calcutta. It was intended to irrigate Moorshedabad and Nuddea, and to enable boats and steamers to avoid much difficult and circuitous delta navigation.

Much was done by Col. Rundall, some years ago, to work out this great scheme, but it is probably hardly in a state to be at once taken up as a well-matured famine relief work.

As regards railways, the Government has already commenced an extension northwards of the Eastern Bengal Railway; this probably is the only large work of the kind which could have any immediate effect in giving work to the starving population of Bengal; but no doubt much will be done to start temporary branches calculated to give cheap and certain transit by rail when the country becomes impassable to carts.

It is said that such lines might be laid down at the rate of many miles per week, at a cost not exceeding 2000*l.* or 3000*l.* a mile; and capable of conversion hereafter into more permanent works, somewhat after the fashion on which the Americans construct their railways in their great alluvial plains. This is a subject which will doubtless be fully considered and acted on, so far as may be practicable.

It may be confidently hoped that the absorbing nature of the present calamity will not divert Lord Northbrook's attention from other quarters to which it had been already directed, and where an early prosecution of designs long since matured may do much to avert future famines.

I will specify only four lines, all of which are ready for immediate commencement, and all of which, had they now been in working order, would have greatly mitigated present anxieties.

One is the line from Ahmadabad, *viâ* Ajmere or Palee, to Delhi. This was an original part of Lord Dalhousie's first great scheme for Indian trunk railways, and ought to have been completed by this time; but it is not yet sanctioned, and a very small portion, which has been made from Delhi southwards, is being constructed on the new metre gauge, which will be a most serious impediment to through traffic. Had this work been commenced when tenders were first made for it by the Bombay and Baroda Company, the effects of the last Rajpootana famine, which is calculated to have cost a million and a quarter of

kind to be done in the way of cleaning tanks, improving water-courses, or making country roads, which would provide the labourers with useful employment near to

---

lives, would have been much mitigated; and few things could do more to avert a repetition of that calamity than an early commencement of this line. But it should be throughout on the standard gauge.

2ndly. A railway from Carwar on the Malabar coast south of Goa, to Hoobly, with an extension into the Southern Mahratta country. This line also is in a state to be commenced without a day's delay; and more than one offer for its construction has been made. It taps a valuable cotton and corn-producing country, the produce of which might be brought to Carwar, one of the few good ports on the coast where ships can load at any time of the year. There would be less objection than usual to making this line on the proposed metre gauge. It will afford to the advocates of that system (of which I have never been one) an opportunity of testing the alleged economy of that construction; and there will be no inconvenience from a break of gauge till the line is extended, as it ought to be, to join the Great Trunk line from Madras to Bombay, somewhere between Bellary and Punderpoor, by which time the question of the gauges ought to be finally settled.

3rdly. An extension of the Great Indian Peninsular Railway, from its terminus at Nagpoor in the central provinces, direct to Calcutta. This would be in every respect a most valuable work, both as opening up old country, and giving access to new.

Its importance to the central provinces is second only to the completion of the plans for rendering the Godavery permanently of use to navigation, a work which has been so long and so unfortunately delayed, and which, it is to be hoped, may at no distant period be resumed.

4thly. A line from Rangoon to Prome, which will doubtless in time be extended to the capital of Burmah. This work also would have been of invaluable service could it have been in operation at the present moment; and had it even been marked out, many thousands of Bengal Coolies, deprived of work in their own country, might have found work upon it, at Burmese wages, which would have afforded a good surplus to their families in Bengal, without sending the working man so far from his home as to the Mauritius or the West Indies.

their own villages, and would add to the resources of the country in time to come. I have no doubt that this kind of work will be largely undertaken; and I hope that a trial, at least, will be made of such small canals as Sir George Balfour has suggested, after the Chinese pattern, for local use. Every district official will have more or less power to set going small and simple works of this kind. Every respectable planter and zemindar, and great numbers of officers who can be spared from their civil or military duties in other parts, will doubtless be sent out into the afflicted district, with power to spend money or grain, with no other restriction than that the work shall be local, and useful, and that the wages shall, as far as possible, be fairly earned and promptly paid.

But how shall the wages be paid? I don't speak of the ultimate expense of payment as a burthen on the Treasury, but as regards the medium. It is an important question whether they should be paid in money or in grain. It will not do to lay down rules too unbending; in one place it may be very expedient to pay in cash; in another it may be mischievous to pay in anything but grain. Indian officials usually understand the principles to be followed in a case like this; and a principle once laid down, the Government may wisely leave much to the discretion of the local authorities, bearing in mind the great maxims,—to keep the people as much as possible in their natural organisation; to use such means, however weak, as may already exist for directing them and managing the distribution of food; to insist, where it is possible, on work being done to earn wages; and above all, to let none die whose death can be prevented.

But the transport, either of money or grain, through a starving population, and over a country where no roads now exist, is not easy. The Lieutenant-Governor and his officers, with a map of the country before them, might do much by using the natural water communications of the country. The stores at Calcutta, or other great commercial centres, may be wisely distributed to local depôts; but they will require guarding there, and will have to be distributed. Sir George Balfour has well illustrated, in a letter lately published, the practical difficulties of distribution.

You will see I have necessarily omitted many essential items from this brief list of the measures which I anticipate may be at once taken. I have said nothing of field hospitals for the diseased, and for the distribution of medicine to the thousands who are certain to be struck down by fever, dysentery, and cholera, when once the famine has lessened their powers of resistance to such maladies; nor have I said a word of the countless orphans who will be left destitute, to be sold, neglected, or cared for, as chance may happen, unless some agency of Government or of charitable interposition step in to save them.

Let anyone read the records of the Irish famine, multiply every difficulty he reads of by five, and he will have a very imperfect idea of what, in the lowest computation, has to be done in Bengal.*

* Before quitting the consideration of what may be done in India, it may not be out of place to quote the following Minute by Sir Thomas Munro, dated the 23rd January, 1824, showing how that great administrator proposed to meet a similar calamity, fifty years ago, in Madras.

"The season is now so far advanced, that every chance of such a fall of rain as could materially improve the state of the crops, is now at an end. The periodical rains have almost entirely failed in all the countries south of Ongole and below the Ghats; and also, though not to so great a degree, in those above the Ghats. We have no means of ascertaining in what proportion the usual produce of the country may

VI.

We now come to what at the present moment is the most important question of all for us here in England to consider. What can we do here to assist in this great work? I have explained to you that the initiative and the executive, of necessity, must rest entirely in India. All the Government here can do is to assure the Viceroy and his officers of their full sympathy and support. This, as you know, has been already done; not that Lord Northbrook needs any assurance on the subject, for I am certain that he knew full well, from the moment that he himself realised the danger, that in meeting it he would receive from his

What can be done in England?

---

have been diminished from this cause, nor do I think that we can expect to gain any very accurate information on the subject. On occasions like the present, all that can be done is to form some probable estimate of the extent of the deficiency. By considering the present market prices, the reports of the collectors on the crops, and other circumstances, I am induced to think that the failure on the whole is not so great as it was in 1807; but that it is not so much less as to justify our neglecting any precautions which may tend to ensure the importation of abundant supplies of grain from Bengal and the Malabar coast. The annual consumption of rice in Madras and its neighbourhood is from ten to twelve thousand garce. [The garce equals about 17¼ English quarters in capacity; in weight it is reckoned at 9256¼ lbs.] The greater part of this quantity formerly came from Bengal, but for the last four years the average importation by sea has only been about seven thousand garce annually, chiefly from Tanjore and the Northern Circars, and a small portion only from Bengal. The importation by land has made up the deficiency in the supply by sea. The whole of the requisite supply has for many years come regularly without any direct encouragement on the part of Government; and I am convinced that the same thing would happen in the present year, and that the market might with perfect safety be left to itself without any other guarantee for its amplest supply than would be afforded by the scarcity price. Were this

Sovereign and country the same entire and cordial support which he would have in waging a war with our deadliest enemy, and that no expense, no trouble, would be deemed too great to preserve from death any of the millions of our fellow-subjects who are threatened with starvation during the coming season in Bengal.

But though the Government here can do but little,

---

question one of mere profit, I should think our not interfering in any way the best course; but when the lives of a great population are at stake, we ought to adopt every measure which may be most likely to avert the approach of famine. Importation may be encouraged, either by a high guarantee price, or by a bounty. In 1807 the members of Government were equally divided on the preference to be given to those two modes, but decided finally in favour of the guarantee price. We have had the advantage of seeing the bad effects which attended the guarantee price; and, as a bounty will, I am satisfied, cause a sufficient importation, without involving us in the difficulties of the management and custody of extensive stores of grain without the means of securing them from fraud and depredation, and without bringing us into the market as grain dealers, I can have no hesitation in giving it the preference to the guarantee price.

"The rate of bounty which I would propose, is thirty rupees per garce on all rice of the description of good cargo rice, which might be imported at Fort St. George from the territories adjacent to Bengal, or from Malabar and Canara, from the 10th February to the 1st June. The whole importation to that period will probably be from ten thousand to fifteen thousand garce, and the expense to Government from three, to four and a half lakhs of rupees (30,000*l.* to 45,000*l.*). If the quantity should not exceed ten thousand garce, it will be unnecessary to continue the bounty after the 1st June, as the ordinary monthly supplies which may be expected till October, will answer all the wants of the market.

"While we endeavour to procure an adequate supply for the present season, we must be careful that we do not, by holding out too much encouragement, overstock the market, as in 1807, so as materially to interfere with the sale of the produce of our own territories in the ensuing year, and thus to distress the Ryots as much in the second year by the want of demand for their produce, as in the first by its failure.

except by supporting the measures initiated from India, I do not say that nothing can be done by England to help.

In the first place, let us avoid confusing the authorities in India by impractical suggestions. We may be sure that what we know they know, and will do to the best of their power. I know of no suggestion which has been offered to the Government here or to any member of it, which has not at once been sent to India, by post or

---

"The whole quantity of rice imported in 1807, was garce 29,010.

	Garce.
Of this quantity the Grain Committee received .	13,798
The Garrison Storekeeper	1,500
Individual Dealers	13,712
	29,010

"The disbursements by the Grain Committee to the 1st January, 1808, were as follows:—

	Garce.
Consignments to the subordinates . . .	1,293
Sales by Auction	27
Sales by Measure	4,253
Sales by Weight	196
	5,769
To the Poor Fund	174
Total garce	5,943

"The above appears to have been all that was issued by Government on account of the scarcity, exclusive of the issues to the troops by the Storekeeper; there was therefore on hand, on the 1st January, 1808,

About garce	7,855
	13,798

which was not required in aid of the scarcity, and if we add to this the probable quantity in the possession of private dealers, there was probably in hand, after the scarcity, a quantity equal to the consumption of Madras for a whole year."

telegram, as its importance seemed to demand. All will, I am sure, receive careful attention, and doubtless, if practicable, will be adopted. But outside the duties of Government is a large area of national duty, which must be undertaken and discharged in the spirit of that feeling which recognises Bengal as being as much an integral part of the British Empire as Cornwall.

The Government will need trustworthy eyes and ears to report, and honest and firm hands to distribute what it has to give, whether in work, wages, or in support of the starving, and there will remain, beyond all that Government can do, an immense field for private charity, far exceeding what can be reached even by the most ungrudging and catholic spirit of English or Indian charity.

We have some thirty-three missionary agencies employed in impressing on the natives of India the truths of Christianity. Can we do better than support this agency in the work which it has always, in former cases of the kind, so willingly undertaken, of feeding the hungry, clothing the naked, healing the sick, and speaking comfort to the dying? Here is a field at once for the energies and means of all who have any portion of missionary spirit, and they will find on the spot an agency which, however scattered and scanty, is yet all-pervading and capable of indefinite extension.

Nor need those who have no faith in such agency sit down in the belief that nothing remains for them to do. The case, as regards the number of helpless, shiftless, human beings who will need succour, even if everything henceforward turns out for the best, is something like that of the late Franco-German war, only infinitely magnified; and no man who has the love of his fellow-creatures strong in him, who has any feeling of patriotism or of human charity, need doubt that there will be an ample field for the most active exertions of all his powers in Bengal during the coming season.

There is only one class that can be superfluous, and that is the aimless idler who might go for want of something better to do. Anyone who goes should have a definite purpose, and provide himself with ample means and some sort of introduction which may enable him at once to place himself in communication with the public authorities, wherever, under the guidance of zemindars or missionary, planter or official, he may find that an intelligent, hard-working Englishmen can be of use.

I say nothing of the means of supplying what funds are needed. They have never been wanting for works of this kind in this great city or in the country at large, and I feel sure that whenever those who usually lead us give the word, the number of those who are ready to obey their call will not be small.

VII.

What can be done to prevent famines hereafter?

But a yet larger question remains to be glanced at. What can be done to prevent famines hereafter? There are many who pretend to know something of India, who will tell you that famine is one of the normal conditions of native life in India, that the East is unchangeable, and that the ordinary laws which we recognise as directing our conduct in this country do not apply in India. I entreat you not to believe a word of this kind of teaching. If I have learnt any one lesson during the many years I have spent in India, it is this: that there is no single law of what we call political economy, or of common sense, which applies to us here in England which is not equally applicable to India. There are, of course, varying conditions, under which these laws are applied, just as the conditions under which such laws act differ in different countries in Europe and in different parishes of this country and of this city. But if the law does not really apply to India, depend upon it, your notion of the law is mistaken, and it is no law at all, but only a delusion.

What, then, are the kind of measures which we may hope to see taken? First of all, Bengal must be organised, and an administration must be provided for it, at least as complete and well linked together from the Viceroy down to the villager, as in other parts of India. This work has been already commenced by Sir George Campbell. It has nothing whatever in it hostile to Lord Cornwallis' permanent settlement. Any incompatibility with the present state of things is due to some non-fulfilment of Lord Cornwallis' intentions and promises.

1. Permanent administrative machinery must be organised for Bengal.

Secondly, you must see that Bengal is provided with ample means of communication. Excellent as is the natural water carriage, it is not really much better or more all-pervading than that which exists in our own country or in Ireland; and yet I need not tell you how imperfect our rivers and estuaries would be as our sole means of communication, and unless they were supplemented by roads, railroads, and canals.

2. Means of internal communication must be provided.

And here arises a question in which the people of England are very directly concerned, for it is through a change in the opinions prevalent in Parliament that the policy of the Government of India has of late been changed. It is not much more than thirty-five years since the want of internal communications in India was recognised by the

Recent changes in English policy as regards providing capital for Indian communications.

Government, and road making, on a considerable scale, commenced. The making of navigable canals and of railways, as general measures, is of still later date. For some years it was agreed that works of this kind ought to be made partly at the expense of the present generation, with such sum as could be spared from the annual revenue after expenses of immediate necessity had been provided for, and that part should be borne by posterity by borrowing the capital which is always so freely lent for such undertakings in England. This system received the sanction of some of the greatest administrators and financiers who have interested themselves in Indian affairs during the present and past generation.

But of late years a school has grown up which has discovered that India is a very poor country, that she is unable to pay more than the most economical provision for hand-to-mouth expenses, and that nothing is to be given for works of permanent improvement unless it can be saved from the current revenue, or the works can be proved, beyond all doubt, to be such as will pay directly an ample percentage of direct earnings. I may mention that this kind of doctrine was, as I understand, affirmed without much discussion or any effectual or peremptory contradiction, by decisions of Parliament, no later than last session. Such, at least, is the reason which is always currently assigned for expending nothing in India unless it can be shown to be immediately and commercially profitable, in the sense of returning, in direct earnings, an immediate interest, more than sufficient to cover the interest which Government, as a borrower, must pay. In fact, the Government must execute its public works in the narrowest spirit of a money-lender;—not of a landowner, or of one who has any permanent interest in the land, or in its cultivators;—not looking to the possible returns ten years hence, still less to indirect returns in the general improvement of the country, calculating no profits save those which can be realised as soon as the work is paid for, and stipulating that those profits must always be something more than the current rate of interest.

How such doctrines are to be reconciled with our principles and practice in building such works as Westminster or London bridges, or the Thames Embankment, or in draining our towns or our fields, or making our highways, I do not pretend to say. If I am wrong in supposing that the doctrine, as above stated, is that which is affirmed by the present English legislature, I shall be very glad to find I have been mistaken. Otherwise, I submit that the question requires further investigation, and I am not doubtful as to the result when once the mind of Parliament is seriously applied to the question.

I have said nothing of what is the greatest safeguard of all against famine in time to come, 3. Works of irrigation and internal navigation. the creation of great works of irrigation and internal navigation, of which many have been devised and some executed by Sir Arthur Cotton and men of his school, and of the other noble schools of engineering which have been formed in India. It is the fashion to deny the facts regarding the results of irrigation works on which Sir Arthur's calculations are based, but I feel certain the more they are tested the more clearly it will be seen that in no other way can money be so advantageously expended, with the view to future production and cheap supply, as in great works of irrigation and internal navigation. Here in England irrigational works naturally occupy a very secondary place in the agriculturist's estimation. But I think the time is not far distant when works of internal navigation will resume the place they occupied in our grandfathers' estimation as the means of conveying the heavy traffic of the country, and when the shade of Brindley may be invoked not only to diminish the cost of living, but the cost of life itself, all along our greatest lines of internal commercial traffic.*

Example of the entire protection of an Indian district from famine by means of effective communication.

I have heard it said, "India is not as England—even with the best means of communication the people will starve when their own crops fail."

I could give many instances to prove the fallacy of this statement. I will give only one, which, however, will probably satisfy you that in India, as in England, actual famine can be prevented by effective means of communication. I select it merely because I know the country well, and can speak from personal knowledge of the facts. The instance I refer to relates to the district between the Godavery and the Toombudrā River, in the Deccan, east of Poona. The tract may be roughly taken at 300 miles in length, from north to south, and 200 miles wide from east to west.

The population consists chiefly of hardy, industrious, intelligent Mahratta cultivators. The country is generally a vast plain, with undulating rocky ridges, and low ranges of bare barren hills, trap rock or trap detritus everywhere forming various soils from rich black cotton soil to shallow red gravel, which only with abundant rain gives a crop of millet, the usual grain. The rains are scanty and uncertain, though the greater rivers rising in the Western Ghauts rarely run entirely dry.

* *Vide* Appendix B.

This district has always been subject to famine whenever there was a serious or repeated failure of the usual rains, or when war or tumult had prevented the timely cultivation of the fields. Ancient Deccan famines.

Tradition tell us of more than one great famine which caused the depopulation of the whole country, and its return to a state of uninhabited jungle. History bears out tradition, and sites of deserted villages are still shown which have never been inhabited "since the great famine."

The people still reckon traditional events by years of scarcity. "It was the year of Holcar's, or Scindia's, or the Mogul's famine," that is, when famine followed the marauding hordes of those great freebooting chieftains, or "The year of the Horse's Nosebag," or, "of the five handsful," meaning years when only a nosebag full, or five handsful of grain, could be bought for the rupee, which in ordinary years would have purchased a hundredweight.

These are expressions I have often heard used by old people in talking of bygone days, and forty years ago traces of recent famine were still to be met with everywhere in the Deccan. More recent Deccan famines.

There had been a severe visitation in 1832 and 1833; traces of its cost to Government in uncollected revenues, and in advances to buy food, were on every public account-book. One of my first experiences in Indian district life was an inquiry into cases where an attempt had been made to wring arrears from the half-starved survivors by actual torture; and famine waifs, in the shape of unclaimed scraps of property which had belonged to unknown fugitives from famine, who had died in their aimless flight from starvation, and children who had been sold by their parents to buy food, or who had been left by dead or starving parents, were to be found at most stations, in the public offices, or in mission houses, or in places of temporary relief which had been provided for the famine-stricken.

Perhaps as striking an instance of the frequency of famine in former and not very distant days as could be found is contained in laws passed, as lately as 1827, to punish slave-dealers. A special exemption is provided for sales of children by starving parents, with a view to save their lives in times of famine.

It so happens that we have graphic notices of the extent and desolating effects of a famine in these districts by three most competent eye-witnesses. Lord Valentia,* who visited the Deccan in 1804, speaks of the harrowing sights he witnessed at every stage as the effects of the "late famine" when twelve thousand people were fed daily at Bombay by the charitable, from stores of rice imported from Bengal. There seem to have been few deaths in the Island of Bombay; but at Panwell, the first station on the mainland, the British officer in charge of the stores calculated the deaths at four thousand in six months, and he had regularly employed twelve men to bury the bodies, which were sometimes found at the rate of from twenty-five to thirty a day. Every halting-place up to Poona had its vision of horror, in the living skeletons too weak even to accept charity, in the bodies—sometimes one hundred in one spot—left a prey to dogs and vultures, and in tales of murder and deadly fights for food, and of children sold and deserted.

The effects were still visible when Sir James Mackintosh visited the same province five years afterwards.

* "Travels," three vols., 4to., London, 1809. Vol. ii. pp. 108 to 199. See also the "Life of Mackintosh," vol. i. p. 466, to the end of the volume.

He and Lady Mackintosh had been active in collecting funds for the famishing in Bombay during Lord Valentia's visit, and Sir James describes the traces of misery and ruin still visible at every place he visited during his tour beyond Poona, and I may add they are not yet quite obliterated. But the most curious testimony of all is borne by the Duke of Wellington, who as Major-General Wellesley saw the district during the worst of the famine in 1803, when, in the campaign preceding the battle of Assaye, he marched his army through it from Mysore, in an expedition which for boldness and true precision in conception, and energy in execution may rank among his greatest exploits. He prepared exactly as he would have done for an expedition into the centre of Arabia, and describes how in the last one hundred and fifty miles, including the famous forced march of sixty miles by which he saved Poona, excepting in one village, he did not see a human creature—so completely was the country desolated by war and famine.*

When I first went to India there were still alive many old men who had a vivid recollection of those times. I remember one, the patel, or head-man of the village of Panowlee, about twelve miles west of Poona, where General Wellesley encamped his cavalry during the monsoon for convenience of water and forage, and to keep open the road to Bombay. The old man pointed out the marks of the lines where "Wesley sahib's" horses were picketted, and said he remembered it well, because he used to be sent with other boys of the better class of villagers to collect the horse litter, which they carefully washed to extract the undigested grains, which in the extremity of famine they, though of good caste, were glad

* *Vide* "Wellington Dispatches," vol. i., p. 508, and following dispatches. Ed. 1838.

to eat. The grain was doubtless some of the Brinjarry stores, the collection of which in the fertile plains of Southern India is noted with such care and forethought in the despatches of the great captain.

Such was the state of the country close to the Peishwas capital seventy years ago. I have said that such things were still possible forty years ago, but I believe they are now as impossible there as here; and why?

In the first place, the ancient Hindoo system which secured a continuous chain of administrative agency from the ruler to the poorest cultivator has been, as far as possible, maintained unimpaired. In the tract I am describing, and far beyond it, in any part of Western and Southern India, the Viceroy can ascertain, by return of post if he pleases, what is the chain of authority through the officials, provincial, local, parochial, down to the village watchman and the poorest cultivator. He could learn equally readily the whole extent of every parish or village, how its lands were cultivated and by whom, the name of every person recognised by law as having an interest in the land, the extent of each man's holding, the number of houses, trades, and professions, and the names of every village authority great and small; and he could convey to any one of them, direct or through the whole chain of authority, any order he wished communicated.

This, remember, is no new device; it is simply a continuation of the old Hindoo system, which may be seen to perfection in any ancient, well-governed Hindoo community, and which was once general all over Bengal, where there now seems some prospect of its being revived; but in the Deccan it has been adopted and incorporated into an English system, and is recognised and provided for by our latest laws passed for that part of the country.

Throughout this tract the Government, as you are aware, are the landlords, but by no means the only ones. The landlords' rights have been parted with by former governments very extensively, and in some of the most fertile and best-managed districts those rights are held to as great or a greater extent by private individuals than by Government. So far from this being an evil, it has always seemed to me to be a great advantage, owing to the healthy competition and variety of interest which it ensures on the landlords' part.

"Ryotwar" system of Western India.

The great distinctive feature of that part of Western India to which I refer, as regards administration of the land revenue, is that Government much more exclusively deals directly with its tenants and sub-tenants than is the case elsewhere. Sometimes it places a chief great or small in the position of representative of Government as landlord. But, as a general rule, every one who holds, and pays for government land, to the extent of one or more fields, deals direct with the Government. This system is often talked of as if it were very complicated and difficult to manage; but such complication and difficulty is only experienced where we have destroyed the native village and district system of administration. Where we have kept up the old village rights, no difficulty or complication whatever is experienced.

Moderation of the Deccan settlement in assessments of rents and land tax at variance with native system of rack renting.

Of course where the customs are such as I have described, it is of the utmost importance to every interest connected with the land that the government charges on the land, whether they might be properly classed as rent or land tax, shall be such as the cultivator can pay, and yet maintain the best system of agriculture known to him.

Now, this is one of the points regarding which the

Deccan settlement officers have departed from, and I think most wisely and judiciously departed from, the native custom which we found in force. The native custom was always to assess a rack rent, and then to make some allowance or annual abatement, as poverty or bad seasons might require. This system worked less oppressively under the native governments than under ours, because the cultivator had always some means of influencing his native ruler, and could to some extent obtain an abatement when needed; but under us, especially where the seasons were precarious, it was found in practice to open the door to over-assessment and grievous oppression, which kept the cultivator always in a state bordering on starvation.

Miserable state of Deccan cultivators in 1834.

When I first knew the Deccan, nothing could exceed the misery and poverty of the great majority of the cultivating classes. Here and there you met a man who by great energy, or by influence with minor government officials, managed to make both ends meet, and perhaps do something more. But, as a general rule, the cultivating classes were deeply in debt —often on the borders of starvation—and, but for their extraordinary attachment to their hereditary lands, and the total absence of other means of living, would probably have very generally abandoned agriculture—or, at least, have fled the country. Yet it is noteworthy that this system of rack renting was one of the last features of their system which the native officials would have willingly abandoned. With a very few brilliant exceptions, I do not remember that I ever met, during the first ten years of my life in India, with a native official who could see the wisdom of moderation in the government demand. And here was an example of one of those cases in which

English views may be wisely and beneficially acted on in matters of this kind, even when they are most opposed to native views.

The school of revenue officers who were trained under Mount Stuart Elphinstone and Sir John Malcolm were all men who shared the opinions of those great statesmen as to the wisdom of moderation in government demands; one of the most active revenue officers in carrying out their views was the late Mr. Williamson Ramsay, to whom I owe my earliest training in Indian revenue matters. In 1835, shortly after I went to India, his then assistant, the late Mr. Henry Goldsmid, discovered a system of oppression, which had been practised in one of the Poona districts, one of the very districts through which the Duke of Wellington had marched thirty years before. The rack rents, pitched according to native custom to suit a year of plenty, though much reduced to suit a year of scarcity, had proved so heavy that they were only extracted from the cultivators by the petty native officials by means of threats of torture, and sometimes by the use of torture itself, in the shape of stones placed on the heads and chests of men standing or lying in the sun, and, as was stated in evidence before us, by threats of running thorns and pounded chilies into the most sensitive parts of their person. Horror-struck by these revelations, Sir Robert Grant, who had just arrived in India as Governor of Bombay, ordered a most searching inquiry; directed that the sums so extorted should be returned to the miserable cultivators, and this inquiry and the repayment of this money was the earliest district duty on which I was employed.

I can give you but a very imperfect idea of the miserable state of the cultivators. Few had more than one meal a day—few more than one coarse blanket and a scrap of cotton cloth as clothing during the year. There were no roads, no wheeled carriages, except that in very rare cases a cart might be seen used for dragging manure to the field, with wheels hewn out of solid stone. The land had no saleable value. Except in a very few cases, where water privileges existed, no manure was ever used. When the rains fell at the proper time there might be a good crop, but everything depended on the rains, and if they failed the country was a desert, and all who could absconded, generally in secret, to the less severely taxed districts of a neighbouring native power, where, though the central government was weak and corrupt, the local officials being resident on the spot, and somewhat interested in the welfare of the people, were generally less exacting, or at any rate more discriminating in exaction, than under the far-reaching and iron despotism of the English Government.

Deccan survey of Goldsmid and Wingate.

Sir Robert Grant commissioned Mr. Goldsmid to revise the Government Assessment of Land Tax, and associated with him Sir George, then Lieutenant Wingate of the Engineers, an officer who to the most benevolent disposition united all the best qualities of head and heart which are found in the officers of our scientific corps. There were few civil officers who could be spared to assist them; but several young military officers, selected chiefly for their knowledge of the Mahratta language, were attached to the Survey; there were some who, like the late Lieutenant Nash of the Engineers, have long since rested in the grave from their labours; some have retired from India, but are still active men in their own native country; others, like Colonels Francis and Cousemaker Anderson, are still employed in the same beneficial work, and all who survive may look back on their labours in the service, however little known or recognised beyond their own provinces, as having contributed, more than anything I know of, to the stability of our rule and the happiness of our subjects in that part of India.

The first operation in these Surveys is to demarcate, measure, and register the area of all lands in a village or parish. The soil is then examined and classified by a separate set of hands; and rates of assessment are fixed by a third and superior class of officers, who, while the measuring and classifying are going on, and are being carefully tested, superintend the operation, and collect all statistical and other data; these enable them to fix, for each class of land, an assessment, which shall not exceed what the past history of the village shows it has been able to pay in average years. This system is repeated in the Deccan, as often as the thirty years leases fall in.

The leading maxims of all the various establishments employed are care, completeness and exactness in registering facts, and moderation in estimating what the government demand shall be. The result of their labours is an immense body of recorded facts — a very perfect Domesday Book, with maps showing every field, and everything necessary to a perfect land register.

The settlements are usually made for periods of thirty years, at the end of which time the lands and registers are re-examined and compared—the incidents of assessment re-adjusted, so as to keep pace with alterations in the prices of produce, and with what Mr. Mill would have called the "indirect increment" of the value of land. As the value of silver has been falling for many years past, or, in other words, as the prices of produce have been rising, the result in the Deccan has been a progressive increase in the government demand on account of Land Tax, though it is still, by comparison, lighter and easier to pay than it was in the best of times under the native government.

As most rights in an Indian village are somehow connected with land, an accurate and complete system of land registry is of the greatest possible use in defining all such rights, and rendering them less liable to be subjects of expensive and needless litigation, and this has been the result whenever the Deccan system has been acted on.

But the care of the first Deccan survey officers did not end with the government assessment. Want of means of internal communication was amongst the most obvious needs of every part of the country at the time that I am speaking of. I believe that at that time, 1834–5, throughout India there could not have been found, away from our great towns, two hundred miles of regularly made and metalled roads.

Road making.

The government mails travelled everywhere throughout India on men's backs or heads, with the exception of some seventy-five miles from Bombay to Poona. Up to this point a mail-cart carried the daily mails along a road very imperfectly bridged, and consequently a very poor facility for wheeled carriages. To the late Sir Robert Grant is due the credit of first making an effectual attempt to introduce into Western India a good system of roads and road-making; and his ideas were taken up with great vigour by the survey officers, who in all their reports pointed out the most prominent needs of the country in this respect. He placed small sums at their disposal, sufficient to mark out and clear roads, whenever it could be done by the labour of the villagers, and larger sums were granted as they could be used for further improvements. At the same time Lieutenant Wingate, with the aid of Lieutenants Gaisford and Davidson, devised a good form of cart, adapted to use in a stony roadless country, and started local factories where village carpenters and smiths were instructed, under competent foremen, in the art of making a workmanlike cart, with iron axles and tires, which had never been used in the agriculture of those provinces before.

Education.

They also directed their attention to education. The village schools were very few and bad; and for the most part but two persons, or at most two families in the village, could read or keep accounts. One was a Brahman—the village priest, astrologer, government accountant, and notary public—for all these offices were usually confined to one Brahman family, in which they were generally hereditary. The other was the village shopkeeper, who was usually at the same time grocer, cloth and grain merchant, pawnbroker and usurer. The latter was often a foreigner from Rajpootana, which seems to have been, from time immemorial, the great nursery of the foreign trading castes for the Deccan. The Marwarry—for he generally came from Marwar—usually appeared in the village with nothing but a rather greasy suit of clothes, of which a huge red turban was always a part, and his writing materials; but he speedily made money; and though he sometimes brought his family and settled, the usual process was that, as he got old and rich, he returned to his native country to build a temple to the God of riches and accounts, whom he assiduously worshipped, in fact, as in metaphor, by once in every year heaping together his account-books, writing-materials, and balance in hand, with lights before the Idol, to be worshipped by him and his household.

With these exceptions, few of what we should call the upper classes, and almost none of the cultivators or lower orders, could read or write, and education for the villagers was consequently as much needed for the protection of the tax-payer as for any other purposes. More than thirty years ago Sir George Wingate submitted to the Government of the day a project of Colonel Davidson's for industrial and other schools, in an ascending series, from the village to the provincial school, which they recommended should be paid for, as well as the roads, by a small percentage on the government land assessment.

This system has only in late years been generally carried out by Mr. Barrow Ellis and others, and is still not so fully developed as its far-sighted projectors intended; but it has succeeded so admirably, and been so much extended, that I trust it may yet do all that they designed for the enlightenment of the agricultural classes in Western India.*

Railways and trunk roads.

In addition to what the land settlement has done for the Deccan, two branches of the Great Indian Peninsula Railway now run through two of its principal divisions; few parts of the tract I began by describing are more than eighty or a hundred miles from a railway station; and there is a considerable network of good roads—not so much as the country requires for a full development of its agricultural resources, but sufficient to protect it against famine. Much also has been done by Colonel Fife and other officers to extend irrigation, by means of works, large and small; and from time to time very

* *Vide* Appendix C.

effective measures have been taken by Government, to encourage and aid the natural disposition of the land-owners to make the utmost use possible of facilities for well-irrigation, which might be still further extended, in most provinces of India, without cost to the State, simply by a liberal policy in fixing the land rents and assessments.

As the net result of all that has been done for the improvement and development of this part of the Deccan, it may be stated, as matter of experience rather than of opinion, that the whole district is fairly protected against the ravages of famine. Scarcity there may be, and often the able-bodied are obliged to go elsewhere in search of work, and to live on imported food; but the population may be pronounced fairly safe against any but occasional isolated deaths from starvation. As a proof that this is not mere theory, I may mention that the seasons preceding 1867 were as nearly rainless, and caused as entire a loss of all crops, and even of the usual supply of grass, as any season which the oldest person in the country could remember, and at one time prices began to rise to a pitch which threatened extreme scarcity and possible famine. But the local rise of prices had its natural effect in attracting grain from without. Considerable supplies were immediately sent to Poona from other neighbouring provinces, and advices sent by telegraph to Kurrachee, Busheir, and Bagdad caused immediate shipment of Punjab, Persian, and Mesopotamian millet and wheat from those ports, the news of which had an instantaneous effect in reducing prices at Poona and its neighbourhood, and the result was that, though the people were straitened, they were fed with imported grain, bought at prices which were above the famine prices of forty years previously, but paid

Net results of improvements in protecting the Deccan from famine.

for by wages earned in Bombay, by the savings of former years, and by money lent on credit to men who were no longer hopelessly in their bankers' debt. None of these things would have been possible without a good revenue settlement fixing and moderating the demands of Government: still less would they have been possible without the railway and the telegraph, and water carriage from far distant ports to Bombay.

I have spoken of these Deccan districts, not because they are solitary instances of what I allege, for I know that I might quote similar cases from every great division of India out of Bengal, and even from Bengal itself; but I cite the Deccan instances because the country was naturally poorer, naturally worse supplied with rain, and naturally more exposed to famine than any part of Bengal; because the measures I have described had their origin in efforts to guard against distress from scarcity; and particularly because there is no single measure to which I have attributed the present practical degree of safety from famine in the Deccan which might not be immediately applied to Bengal itself; and I cannot but think that, if the present distress and suffering leads to the application of what I believe to be effectual remedial measures, the great calamity which we apprehend may prove to be the greatest blessing which has been conferred on Bengal since we have known the country.

System equally applicable to Bengal.

"But," I have been frequently told, "this system is all very well for the sparsely-peopled Deccan; it is utterly inapplicable to densely-peopled Bengal, and would be at variance not only with the habits of the people, but with the rights treated by the permanent settlement."

To this I answer by referring to the district of

Guzerat, as densely peopled as Bengal—far richer, better cultivated, and with tenures more complicated, and land frequently more subdivided, than Bengal.

The task of applying to Guzerat the system of minute land registry and valuation, which is the foundation of the Deccan settlements, has been found more difficult and delicate, of course, than in the Deccan, but by no means impossible. All that I have said of its benefits and success in defining rights, in preventing litigation, in raising at one and the same time the value of land and the amount of land revenue, might have been said with equal truth of Guzerat, but the example would not be so striking because of the greater natural advantages of Guzerat in soil, climate, population, and water communication by sea. The system has since been extended, and with equally good results northward to Sind, southward to Mysore, and eastward to the Berars. I do not say always with uniform ease and success, because its great principles of moderation, and respect for established rights have, perhaps, not always been equally well remembered, and wherever they have been departed from, there success has been less complete; but, wherever the original characteristic features of moderation, respect for all vested rights, and careful adjustment to local peculiarities have been preserved, no difficulty whatever has been experienced in introducing it.

It is as popular with the cultivators and landowners, great and small, as with the government officials, for the simple reason that its object is to ascertain and preserve all rights pertaining to the land, and that it is as much in the interest of the proprietor as of the cultivator, as much for the protection of the tax-payer as for the convenience of the tax-gatherer, to see its provisions fairly carried out.

APPENDIX A.

The facts of the impending calamity in Bengal, as ascertained by the government officials, and the mode in which the Government there proposes to meet it, cannot be better understood than by a perusal of the resolutions of the Viceroy and of the Lieutenant-Governor, dated the 5th and 8th of November, the full text of which has been received since the foregoing remarks were written. They are as follows :—

Resolutions by H. E. the Viceroy and Governor-General of India.

Fort William, 7th November, 1873.

The periodical reports of the state of the crops, published in the *Calcutta Gazette*, have shown that the autumn harvest of rice will fail to a large extent in many districts of the provinces of Bengal and Behar, and that in some districts of the province of Behar especially there is reason to fear that the harvest of the coming spring will partially fail also. These prospects may yet be modified for the better, or for the worse, by the condition of the weather during the next three months.

2. The Lieutenant-Governor of Bengal brought these grave circumstances to the notice of the Government of India at the earliest possible moment. No time has been lost in devising, in concert with his Honour, the measures and the policy best adapted to avert the distress which threatens extensive and populous tracts of country;

for it is certain that such losses must occur as will cause severe pressure on some classes of the population in many districts, during a period of several months.

3. As some little time must elapse before the extent of the evil can be fully known, the conduct to be pursued by the Government cannot at present be exactly decided. But the Governor-General, fully recognising the advantage of publicity on such an occasion, will state the views and intentions of the Government of India so far as they can now be determined.

4. Various suggestions have been received to the effect that the Government should interfere with the trade in grain, either by prohibiting the exportation of this most important article, or by undertaking the general purchase and distribution of it throughout large tracts of country, or by regulating in some manner the prices of it in the markets. Without making any pledge as to what may or may not be done, in the event of extreme necessity arising which cannot now be foreseen, the Government is not prepared to adopt any such measures, and would always avoid them so far or so long as they could possibly be avoided.

5. The Governor-General has full confidence that the energy and enterprise of those engaged in the internal trade of British India will prove equal to the occasion, and that supplies (excepting under the conditions to be noticed hereafter) will generally be at hand to meet any deficiencies of grain in different parts of the country.

6. It has been officially reported that on the very first appearance of the prospect of a short autumn harvest, large quantities of grain were imported into the trade centres of Behar, and much evidence has since been received to the effect that grain is being despatched by the merchants without any delay or hesitation to the principal marts in the districts likely to be affected by scarcity. The Governor-General is sanguine that the

same commercial activity will prevail wherever it is needed, and that it will become greater and greater, according as the demand for it may be intensified.

7. It has, however, been proved, by the sad experience of famines in India, that exceptional circumstances may arise whereby numbers of persons may be exposed to danger of starvation, or to disease arising from want of food. In all such cases, where human life may be at stake, the Government and its officers will do their utmost to apply the most effectual remedy that may be practicable, and will strive, by forethought and management, to prevent the occurrence of any such misfortunes.

8. There are certain respects and particulars in which the Government, while abstaining from interference with the ordinary course of trade, can render assistance towards mitigating the effects of scarcity.

9. In the first place the opportunity will be taken to prosecute with vigour the execution of public works in those districts where large numbers of persons are, or will soon be, in need of employment or in distress.

10. Orders have been given by the Government of India to enlarge the operations on the canal from the river Soane, and to begin the Northern Bengal (State) Railway in anticipation of the sanction of the Secretary of State, for both which works plans and estimates are ready, which works, too, will be carried on in the midst of the districts where want of employment must be most felt, and are calculated to benefit the country generally, and especially to prevent or lessen the occurrence of scarcity in future.

11. The Lieutenant-Governor of Bengal has been authorized to begin immediately such public works (in addition to those already in progress) as can be usefully undertaken in distressed districts, whether from funds granted by the Government of India, or from provincial funds, or from local resources.

12. The requirements for labour on all these public works will afford employment to large numbers who by reason of the cessation or the slackness of the usual agricultural operations in a season of scarcity, may be thrown out of work.

13. Thus considerable bodies of men will be congregated on, or near the works at a distance from their homes, and often in localities remote from the established markets. It will be necessary, therefore, that sufficient supplies of food be collected for their sustenance. If the accumulation of such supplies be left to the ordinary course of commerce, special pressure will be put on the grain trade in certain localities at the very time when all its resources are being taxed for the general supply of the province or district. And if the wages were to be paid in cash to so large an aggregate of labourers, an extraordinary rise of prices would be created by the action of Government, thereby aggravating the crisis in districts already placed in critical circumstances, and so far counteracting the benefit which the works were intended to secure, namely, the mitigation of the effect of the scarcity.

14. Now, in regard to those public works carried on under the orders either of the supreme Government or of the local government, the State will be in the position of an employer of labour on an unusually large scale, and is justified in doing that which all other employers do, namely, selecting the mode of remunerating its work-people most acceptable to them, and most suitable to the surrounding circumstances. Such mode of remuneration will generally be payment in kind; that is, in food grain. For this particular purpose, then, sufficient supplies of grain will be purchased and laid in, both by the Government of India and by the local government, for the public works under their charge respectively. These supplies will be obtained in such a manner as to interfere as little

as possible with the trade in grain, and with the supplies of food ordinarily available for consumption in the neighbourhood of the works, or within the area of the distressed districts. The Governor-General relies on the carefulness of the local government in making provision with this view. For the works to be carried on from imperial funds, the supreme government has resolved, in regard to its liability for the maintenance of the labourers, to arrange for obtaining supplies from provinces beyond the limits of the territories affected by the failure of the crops in Bengal and Behar. The Government of Madras and the chief commissioner of British Burmah have accordingly been requested to make purchases gradually, through the agency of the trade, for this purpose.

15. The future arrangements for the supply of food grain for the labourers on the public works will be strictly limited according to the requirement and to the purpose in view.

16. Besides the works just described, which are to be undertaken by the Government, there are many public improvements which can be undertaken, either by corporations or other bodies, such as municipalities and trusts. For loans of money from the Government Treasury to such corporations, ample provision is made by Act XXIV. of 1871 (the Local Public Works Loan Act). In some cases, under the rules recently promulgated in accordance with the Act, the Lieutenant-Governor is competent to make the loans on his own authority, from funds which have been allotted for that purpose by the Government of India. In those cases where, under the rules, the sanction of the Government of India is necessary, any judiciously matured project, any well-considered application, which may be recommended by the local government, will meet with the immediate approval of the Government of India. If the rules in respect to preliminary inquiry and the like shall be deemed by the Lieutenant-Governor to cause

delay, which may be prejudicial at a critical time, his Honour is authorized to relax them temporarily.

17. For agricultural improvements, the Land Improvement Act (XXVI. of 1871) provides for advances of money being made by Government to any landlord or tenant desiring to make an improvement in any land of which he is in possession or occupation. The improvements specified in the Act—that is, wells, tanks, and other works for the storage and distribution of water; works for draining, reclaiming, clearing, and enclosing lands—are well suited for employing the labour which may be unemployed in the villages by reason of the stoppage of ordinary work in the fields. The Governor-General earnestly hopes that many landlords will take advantage of the provisions of the Act. The rules under this Act recently promulgated by the local government, with the sanction of the Government of India, contain many precautionary provisions which are necessary in ordinary times, but which at a time of urgency might cause undesirable delay. The Lieutenant-Governor is authorized to make such relaxation of the rules as his Honour may deem advisable, under the circumstances of the districts affected by the drought.

18. In reference to the local works, the Governor-General desires that the levy of the road cess may be postponed in any district, or portion of a district, where the Lieutenant-Governor may consider that the cess-payers are in distress. It is to be remembered that, in those districts which are not so severely affected, the proceeds of the road cess will afford the means of usefully employing any surplus labour that may be thrown upon the market.

19. In the next place, the Government may contribute something towards facilitating the transport of grain in the interior of the country. The agents, therefore, of the guaranteed railway companies whose lines traverse Bengal

and Behar, have been authorized to reduce by one-half the rates charged for the carriage of grain despatched to the districts affected by scarcity, the Government undertaking to reimburse the companies for the difference thus caused in the traffic receipts. The precedent is followed which was established by the adoption of a similar course in 1869.

20. The Governor-General is sure that the private steam-flotillas on the principal rivers, and the native craft which are so abundant throughout the river system of Bengal, will bear a most useful part in the conveyance of grain to the places where it is urgently needed.

21. In those places where the means of water-carriage do not exist, the grain-traders must mainly depend on the country carriage. There may, indeed, be ground for apprehension that, as the dry season advances, mortality beyond the average must arise among the draught cattle. This subject will doubtless receive the anxious consideration of the local government and of its officers. Every aid that can be afforded by the commissariat or other public departments will be rendered; and inquiries are being made as to the practicability of constructing tramways in the distressed districts.

22. Should the distress become severe, and should the worst anticipations be realised, the Government will assist in the formation of relief committees, and in the organisation of a system of relief for those who, despite all the operations of trade, may be threatened with death or disease from want of food. The Governor-General is sure that the private benevolence, which has always been conspicuous in India, will be evoked on this occasion, according as the need for its exercise shall become apparent. A central relief committee will, as soon as the local government shall consider it to be necessary, be formed at Calcutta, as the capital of the provinces under the jurisdiction of the Lieutenant-Governor of Bengal. To this

committee will be entrusted the general administration of the funds for relief which may be received from private sources and from the Government, and the distribution of those funds among the relief committees which the Lieutenant-Governor will establish in the districts affected by scarcity. The district relief committees will distribute assistance to the distressed, either in cash or in grain, or in prepared food, according to the instructions which they may receive from the local government. Any purchases of grain which may be necessary will be made either by the central committee or by the district committees. If the committees lay in supplies of grain they will be instructed to do so in the manner best calculated to avoid undue interference with the ordinary course of trade, or with the stores available for consumption in the neighbourhood.

23. The Governor-General relies upon the Lieutenant-Governor to take steps for organising these district and local committees in seasonable time, and in sufficient number, so that the measures for relief shall be far reaching and comprehensive in proportion as the distress may become wide-spread. What application his Honour may make for assistance from the ranks of the public service with a view to effectively constituting these committees, will receive immediate attention from the Government of India.

24. Inasmuch as the prevalence of want may give rise to many forms of epidemic disease, the augmenting and the reinforcing of the medical staff of all grades in the afflicted districts will be of primary importance. Any assistance which the Lieutenant-Governor may require in this respect from the Government of India will be duly accorded.

25. The Governor-General is sure that non-official gentlemen, both European and native, resident in the districts affected by scarcity, will come forward to serve

on the relief committees, and will render that assistance which has proved so valuable on former occasions of a like nature.

26. Furthermore, non-official gentlemen, European and native, zemindars, landlords, planters, and others may at once render much service by undertaking the provision and distribution of grain, in localities where, from the difficulty of transport, the absence of traders, or other local circumstances, food cannot, during the period of scarcity, be obtained by the people. In such cases, the Government will be prepared to grant advances of money to non-official gentlemen who may undertake to import grain from a distance, and to distribute it at prices to be regulated according to the circumstances of the case. The condition that such grain be imported from distant places, so that the ordinary operations of the local trade may not be interfered with, must be observed. Accounts of the advances will be submitted to and passed by the local government; and any loss or charge which may arise upon the operations will, of course, be borne by the State.

27. The Governor-General is confident also that many landholders, recognising the duty towards their tenants, their dependents, and their destitute neighbours, which is morally imposed upon them by the possession of property, will, of their own accord and from their own resources, dispense relief in the manner which they may deem to be most effectual.

28. The Governor-General feels assured that the Lieutenant-Governor is well aware of the necessity for preparing the local arrangements for relief beforehand; that is, before the emergency shall have actually befallen the districts in question, before the intensity of the trouble shall have begun to be felt, so that the distress may not attain such proportions that the local authorities cannot adequately deal with it, or make such progress that they cannot overtake it.

29. Hereafter, as the season shall draw near for the sowings of the next harvest, the Government will be prepared to authorize advances of money to landlords or tenants for the purchase of seed-grain wherever the Lieutenant-Governor may consider such a measure to be desirable.

30. It is to be hoped that, in the populous tracts visited or threatened by distress, unemployed labourers may emigrate to places where food is in comparative plenty, where a special demand exists for their labour, where culturable waste abounds, such as the tea-districts, the Doars, the provinces of Assam, and of British Burmah. If it be found possible for the Government to facilitate such emigration, directly or indirectly, the Governor-General will be glad to receive any suggestions which the Lieutenant-Governor may be able to make.

31. Having given such instructions as seemed to be called for at the present time, the Governor-General requests that the Government of Bengal will transmit periodically at short intervals to the Government of India full reports on the state and prospects of the crops, the stock of food, so far as it can be ascertained, the public works in progress, the relief operations, if any, and all other circumstances relating to the scarcity. Together with these reports there should be forwarded the opinions of the district officers, formed on the most recent data obtainable. The Governor-General is satisfied that these opinions will be given fully, unreservedly, and promptly, even though time may not have admitted of their being precisely elaborated, and though they may be subject to subsequent correction and verification. Full information on these matters will be published from time to time.

32. Lastly, the Governor-General places full reliance upon the foresight and the energy of the Lieutenant-Governor of Bengal to provide for and to cope with the difficulties which may spring from the drought and

scarcity; and upon the zeal and experience with which his Honour's efforts will be seconded by the officers of all grades and branches of the public service. He feels the responsibility which devolves on the Government of India under the present circumstances, and he trusts, that with God's blessing, the measures to be adopted will prove successful in averting, so far as may be humanly possible, the calamitous effects of the drought.

Resolution of Government of Bengal.

Dated Calcutta, 3rd November, 1873.

Read a Resolution of the Government of India, Public Works Department, No. 431 B.C., dated the 28th October, 1873, on the subject of the provision of work in these provinces for the people who may be thrown out of employment by the expected failure of the crops in many districts.

1. The Lieutenant-Governor is pleased to direct the publication of this Resolution.

2. Orders for carrying out the instructions of the Government of India, in regard to the Soane Canal and Northern Bengal Railway works, will be issued in the proper departments.

The Gunduck Embankment scheme is one which involves very difficult considerations, but it will be again carefully examined.

The proposed lowering of the railway fares has been arranged.

3. As regards works other than those above-mentioned, the Lieutenant-Governor has received full authority to undertake such relief works as may seem to be necessary in various parts of the country. His view is that, to render effectual aid to the people, it is of all things most necessary that work should be offered in good time, so

that the existence of public works may be known to the people at large, and those who stand in need of work may find their way to the work, and be suitably provided for, before the greatest stress comes. All experience shows that work is wanted to avert starvation rather than to save people already half-starved and unfit for work, and that it takes time to draw to public works people who are not accustomed to labour for hire. In this view, in case of reasonable apprehension of scarcity, we can hardly begin too soon.

4. The Lieutenant-Governor also believes that there can be no sure test of the state of the country—no barometer, as it were, by which the condition of the people can be better gauged—than the degree to which they seek employment on public works. As such works are found more and more to attract classes usually self-supporting, so we may judge that there is want in the country; that is, provided that this test is established in sufficient time.

5. It is impossible yet to tell the degree to which there may be scarcity in the country. We yet trust to the mercy of Providence to avert the worst. But there can be no doubt that, unless there is some very decided improvement in present prospects, there will be such shortness of crops that as soon as all hope of further employment in watering crops still alive, and sowing cold-weather crops comes to an end, the need for employment will be much greater than usual. The immediate course, then, which the Lieutenant-Governor has thought best, is to extend and enlarge the scope of the usual district works undertaken at this season in various parts of each district. He has already settled schemes of such works with the commissioners of Patna and Bhaugulpore, and has authorized the local officers to undertake them and carry them on, wherever and whenever there is a demand for employment. In every part of the country, where

the condition seems to be such as to render the need of employment probable, works will be opened and employment offered. It will not be attempted in such cases to draw together foreign labour by any extraordinary means, but all labour locally offering will be accepted. The works (so far as beyond ordinary means and requirements) are undertaken in order to give labour: we do not seek labour for the sake of the works. The local officers have been assured that if the labour thus employed absorbs their local means, these will be supplemented from the general treasury.

6. General instructions, in the spirit of those given to the commissioners of Patna and Bhaugulpore, have also been given by the Lieutenant-Governor to the commissioners of Rajshahye and Burdwan, and all commissioners are now authorized to act in the spirit of these instructions wherever there may be need of such measures.

7. The Northern Bengal Railway runs through districts where there has been the greatest failure of rain, and where there is the greatest apprehension regarding the crops; but the people of those districts are wholly unaccustomed to labour for hire, and it may be doubtful whether they will go far from their homes for work till they are very hard pressed indeed. It may be a question, then, whether we can rely on a single line of railway for the relief of that country generally. Deeming that roads connecting the various parts with the railway—feeder roads as they are usually called—are a necessary part of the railway system, the Lieutenant-Governor proposes to spread more widely the opportunities of employment by undertaking at the same time roads leading to the principal railway stations. The civil authorities will at once set themselves to devise the lines which will best subserve the traffic of the country, and the engineering staff of the Northern Bengal Railway will be requested to

lay out and superintend these lines, which may connect the railway with the Berhampooter river system on the one side, and with the Mahanuddee on the other.

8. The note of the Lieutenant-Governor, published in the supplement to the *Gazette* of the 10th September, 1873, explained his Honour's views regarding the great importance of improving the means of communication between the populous district of the west and the insufficiently-peopled districts of the east, and pointed to a scheme of roads from west to east. The north-eastern portion of the Tirhoot district, and the north part of Bhaugulpore by which such roads would pass, is the very country where the people will be most in need of employment, and these roads should certainly be undertaken at once. Durbhangah may be taken as the point of departure, from roads already made, of the great Behar populations which tend to the east in search of labour. Fortunately Mr. Stevens, the able and energetic engineer of the Durbhangah Estate, is well acquainted with this country, and has already devised the lines of road which he thinks the best. The Lieutenant-Governor has arranged with the commissioner of Patna and Mr. Stevens, that the latter officer should lay out two lines from Durbhangah to the Koosee river, one in the direct line to Purneah, and the other by Natpore to the north towards Titaliya. The commissioner of Bhaugulpore is to arrange for the junction of these two lines with Purneah and Titaliya. From Purneah the present metalled road leads to Dengraghat, on the Mahanuddee; whence to Dinagepore a line of road is already marked out, which will be taken up as a relief work. From Titaliya the road to Julpigoree may be improved, and thence there is a line by Cooch Behar to the Berhampooter. By these lines, and others in connection with the Northern Bengal Railway, complete means of communication from west to east will, it is hoped, be established north of the Ganges. Further to

the south, the line from Rajmehal to Dinagepore should also receive attention.

9. In Burdwan a work already discussed, viz., the connection of the Damoodah with the Kana Nuddee has already been put in hand, partly in the hope of obtaining an immediate supply of water, and partly in order to give employment.

In this same part of the country there has been much complaint of the want of good tanks for drinking-water, of petty drainage channels, and such like improvements. There can be no doubt that petty works of this kind are at least as useful as larger works, and they certainly bring employment more effectually to the homes of the people. But, on the other hand, it would be impossible for Government to undertake and superintend such works of local improvement on private property. The Lieutenant-Governor has, however, instructed the commissioner to ascertain whether it might be arranged that private landlords should undertake such works, Government, if necessary, advancing the money on the security of the estates. He feels sure that if the upper classes feel the duties of their position, such an arrangement should be gladly accepted by them, and be very feasible.

10. The Lieutenant-Governor feels sure that he may trust to the zeal and energy of the local officers to give effect to these orders, and that, whatever need may arise, they will not be found wanting. He feels that he can count on the thorough assistance of the European settlers. He would also express the earnest hope that the officers of Government will have the aid and co-operation of the native landholders, and generally of those classes of natives whose wealth, influence, and position may enable them to contribute to the duty of assisting their poorer fellow-countrymen. The most effective work cannot be done without that assistance.

APPENDIX B.

Since this Lecture was written, I have met with the following remarks in an able pamphlet published by a practical authority on such questions, who puts the results of recent irrigation works so concisely that I cannot do better than quote him.*

He first cites the following remarks of Colonel Chesney:—

"But the surpassing value of irrigation in India is to be found in the insurance it effects against the horrors of famine. Twice within the last thirty years have the rains failed in the plains of the Upper Ganges. For the last seven years Western India has suffered under the calamity of successive deficient harvests, producing an enormous rise of prices, which would, with a less frugal race, have caused extreme distress. The great famine of 1866, although experienced in greatest intensity in Orissa, extended, with more or less severity, from the Ganges to the extreme south of the peninsula, and the sufferings which it created must have been undergone by from fifty to sixty millions of persons. In 1869 a large part of India was again afflicted with extreme drought, producing, in many extensive regions, all the miseries of famine, and involving a large public outlay to keep the starving poor alive. It is to prevent, or, at any rate, to alleviate, the effects of these awful calamities, that irrigation works are needed in India. Even as an insurance against the direct loss of the land-revenue, which must

* "Famines in India; their Remedy and Prevention. A Paper read by Wm. Tayler, Esq. (late Commissioner of Patna), before the East India Association, on Thursday, December the 18th, 1873."

necessarily be foregone when the people have no crops to sell, such works are at once extraordinarily remunerative to the State. The famine of 1837–8 involved a direct loss of 500,000*l.* sterling on this head; the Ganges Canal is estimated to have prevented at least as much during the famine of 1861. Yet the direct saving in land-revenue is obviously only a part of the saving which thus accrues. A great calamity of this kind cannot fall on a country without paralysing the whole course of trade and business, and the effect must necessarily make itself felt in every branch of the national revenue. The loss of public revenue, again, is but small compared with the destruction of national wealth resulting; and this it must be the duty of the Government, as representing the interests of the general community, so far as possible, to prevent. And, after all, the loss of wealth, whether public or private, is surely but the lowest ground on which to base the argument for active measures. The prevention of the miseries of famine should alone be a sufficient, as it ought to be the leading, motive to action. It is not as if the affair were a speculative one, and that the question were one of possible calamities and doubtful remedies. Droughts have occurred in India so frequently that their occurrence before long, in some part or other of the country, is reasonably to be expected; and famine, as the certain effect of drought, *can be prevented by irrigation.* Here, then, is clearly one of the most important duties that can be placed before the government of any state. The task is one that only the Government can undertake; for it is not merely to carry out projects which promise to be remunerative in the ordinary sense of the word, it is to extend irrigation, wheresoever irrigation may be possible, throughout the country. Till that is done, and the danger of famine has been guarded against to the fullest possible extent, the English in India may replace anarchy by peace, and may distribute equal justice, and remove ignorance; but it cannot be said that they fulfilled their whole duty by the people of the country."

He then quotes information furnished to him by Sir Arthur Cotton, regarding the principal irrigation works now in progress in different parts of India, beginning with Tanjore, the Delta of the Cauvery, where there had been from ancient times an extensive system of irrigation.

In 1827 there was great alarm about the state of the district, and a new system of works was commenced in 1830. During forty-three years 200,000*l.* or 300,000*l.* have been spent on the works, and there has not only been no famine in the Delta, but it has constantly supplied neighbouring districts in times of scarcity.

The annual revenue has during that time increased from 420,000*l.* in 1830 to 720,000*l.* at present, an increase of 300,000*l.* a year, the greater portion directly or indirectly due to improved irrigation. This increase of annual revenue represents a capital of five millions sterling, and the benefit to the cultivator is about five times that which goes into the treasury.

On this point Sir Arthur Cotton truly says—

"In estimating the results of capital invested by Government in public works, the first point always is, What is the total direct return in money to the community? and quite a secondary one, What are the direct or indirect returns into the Treasury? It is of the utmost importance that this should be always kept in view. The case is quite different from that of a private speculation.

"In that case if a work does not return a fair interest to the investors, whatever the public benefit may have been, it is a loss to the company. But if, through any circumstances, a work does not return net 5 per cent. to Government, but at the same time benefits the people to the extent of 20 or 30 per cent., it is really an immense benefit to the country and even to the treasury, because it is impossible to enrich the people without all the different items of the revenue increasing."

These canals were not adapted for navigation, which of course would have greatly added to their value, and navigation has been attended to in the irrigation works of the Godavery Delta, which are still incomplete, only 480,000 acres being as yet irrigated out of about one million irrigable in the Delta. The complete Godavery works are estimated to cost one million sterling; this will provide 700 miles of navigable canal with locks 120 feet long by 20 wide. The increase of produce is estimated at 2*l.* per acre for a single crop, which will give 200 per cent. on the outlay, besides cheap transit. The saving of canal transit as compared with cart hire is estimated at threepence a ton a mile, which would give another 90 per cent. on the outlay, if only 100,000 tons a year are carried on an average, besides the cheapened and improved passenger transit. Sir Arthur adds:—

"Again, the price of rice is expected to rise to 1½*d.* a lb. in Bengal, and allowing 1,200 lb. as the produce per acre, and 1¼*d.* for value of rice, deducting carriage to Bengal, one crop would be worth 6*l.*, or *six times the whole cost of all the works*, so that in a famine year the whole would be paid six times over by a single crop. This would give some idea of the utter insignificance of the costs of these works compared with their effects. With respect to the returns to Government, the water-rate now paid is 4 rupees per acre, or 40 per cent. on the cost of the works, besides tolls and the increase of the taxes.

The total increase of the revenue of the district has been from 220,000*l.* to 520,000*l.*, or nearly 140 per cent., 300,000*l.* on an outlay up to this time of 600,000*l.*, 50 per cent. Certainly almost the whole is due directly and indirectly to the works. Thus, in respect of direct returns to Government, this is perhaps the most profitable engineering work in the world, excepting the adjoining district works—those of Kistna. With reference to famine, there has not been the smallest fear of the district for the twenty-five years since the works were begun, and it secures a vast extent of the surrounding country, and it will, I hope, produce no inconsiderable supply for the distressed districts in Bengal this season. And these works yet admit of a further improvement. Though there is water in the canals all the year, yet they cannot nearly be kept full in the dry season. If water were stored in the Upper Godavery, not only would 500 miles of that river and the Wurdah be kept in an effective state for navigation in the dry season, but the water would be of great value in the Delta, both for improved navigation, and for extension of the second crop cultivation. This water could be supplied at a very moderate cost. But without this, if 1,000,000 acres are irrigated, the water rate alone will be 400,000*l.* a year, and with the increase in other taxes, there will be a revenue of 750,000*l.* a year, and this district, one of the lowest in India in revenue, will be at the head of all the districts of India. The fact to be considered is, that, not only has famine been prevented, but the increase of produce on a million of acres will be 2,000,000*l.* a year, and another 1,000,000*l.* will be saved in transmit, making an increase of wealth of 3,000,000*l.* a year, in one district out of about two hundred, while the whole of the taxes paid by it would be 750,000*l.*; so that abolishing all taxes would be a small boon compared with these works, for which the people in the district have paid nothing, the increase of wealth being four times the whole amount of taxation. If the same were done in all districts, it would add 600,000,000*l.* a year to the wealth of India, *fifteen times* the whole amount of taxes, omitting the opium revenue, which is not paid by India.

"*Kistna District.*—This is exactly a similar case to that of Godavery. The works were projected by Colonel Lake, of Kars. The expenditure has not been so great; indeed, I believe, up to this time, not much more than half that of Godavery, or about 300,000*l.*, while the increase of produce per acre is estimated higher there on account of the superior fertility of the soil, owing no doubt to the Kistna flowing through a limestone country. By the last return I have seen 200,000 acres were watered, giving an increase of perhaps 2*l.* 10*s.* per acre, or 500,000*l.* a year, 170 per cent. on the outlay, besides cheap transit. But the works are in a much more backward state than those of the Godavery. They have now also recommenced upon these works, and are carrying them out vigorously. When completed, the results will be fully equal to those of the Godavery. The returns to Government are much higher than those of the above district, for the total increase of revenue is nearly or quite equal to the Godavery. The direct returns in water rate on 200,000 acres at 4 rupees, 80,000*l.*, is 27 per cent., besides tolls."

Sir Arthur very justly comments on the grievous shortsightedness and false economy of not completing these works as rapidly as possible, and adds—

"The increase on the whole of these two Delta works is as follows:—

Revenue of tract now forming Godavery and Kistna Districts before the works . .	£503,000
Ditto average of last two years, 1872-73 . .	1,065,000
Increase . . .	£562,000

"The expenditure to this time is 900,000*l.*, on which the increase is 60 per cent. Or the increase represents a capital of 10,000,000*l.*, more than ten times the cost of the works. These are the returns to the Treasury.

"*The Toombuddra Works.*—These are the Madras Irrigation Company's Works; they have cost 1,500,000*l.*, and are now in a complete working state; but as yet only a small extent of land has been watered, through a combination of circumstances, the principal of which I am satisfied is the Government refusing to let the Company manage their own affairs and sell the water themselves. I believe this year not more than 20,000 acres, yielding 12,000*l.*, will be watered. But the project is a perfectly sound one. There is water sufficient to irrigate 400,000 acres of rice, which at an increase of produce of 2*l.* 10*s.* per acre, would be 1,000,000*l.* a year, or 65 per cent., besides the navigation of 190 miles of main canals, which if it conveyed only 100,000 tons a year would cause a saving at 3*d.* a ton a mile, or 240,000*l.* a year, or 15 per cent. additional, besides the benefits of passenger transit. Thus there is nothing wrong in the project itself, and it is certain that before long the water will be fully used. The returns to the Company would then be at 6 rupees an acre, 240,000*l.* a year, or 15 per cent. gross, besides tolls. The cost has been about 4*l.* per acre. The canal is led through a most fertile tract of country.

"*The Orissa Works.*—These works have cost about 1,250,000*l.* up to this time, but they are not nearly completed. They have cost about 3*l.* 10*s.* per acre, and the increase of produce is estimated at 1*l.* 10*s.* per acre, which would be 40 per cent., besides navigation. These works also have been stopped, or nearly so, though there is something doing now. But here they have had to contend with a real difficulty, which had not been thought of, that is, the people being of so low a type that they have not used the water to any extent yet. The evil influence of the zemindars has greatly helped this. No doubt the difficulty will be got over before long. Had the people used the water this year, the crop on 350,000 acres would have been worth, at the famine price, 7*l.* 10*s.* an acre, 2,500,000*l.* sterling, or nearly double the whole cost of the works. The most grievous mistake of all these works has been the not completing the canal communication with Calcutta, which would at this critical time have carried all their surplus produce and that from the fertile districts of the Upper Mahanuddee to the famine districts.

"*The Soane Works.*—This great project, to cost ultimately nearly 4,000,000*l.*, has been vigorously carried on, and is happily so far advanced as to enable them just now to admit the water into the canal and carry life to a considerable tract of country—the one bright gleam in the dark prospect before us. I have heard of 30,000 acres being watered, and a great deal more has been reached by this time. I am in hopes that 100,000 acres will be watered this season, yielding 50,000 tons of grain, and saving the lives of half a million of people. About 750,000*l.* have been spent, I believe, as yet on these works. They ought to water 1,500,000 acres at least, yielding an increased produce of 2,250,000*l.*, or 60 per cent., besides navigation. A most important part of this project is that the main canal will form a part of the grand artery of water communication up the Valley of the Ganges from Allahabad to the head of the proposed Rajmahal Canal, 450 miles. The value of this work will be perfectly incalculable. There would certainly be a traffic on it of 2,000,000 tons, which, at a saving of only a ¼*d.* compared with the river, would be 900,000*l.* a year on goods alone, or 22 per cent. on the cost. And there would be several hundred miles of navigable branches besides. Had this communication from Calcutta all the way to the Ganges Canal now been open, it would have essentially altered the whole face of the question of the famine, conveying any amount of grain at a nominal cost both from the North-West and from Calcutta, and so from all the world, through the very heart of the threatened districts, the branch canals distributing it throughout the tract.

"*The Ganges Canal.*—This work has cost about 2,500,000*l.*, and waters now nearly 1,000,000 acres, yielding an increase of produce at 1*l.* 10*s.* per acre of 1,500,000*l.*, at 60 per cent. besides the navigation. The returns in money, at Rs. 2½ per acre, are about 200,000*l.* at present, or 8 per cent. gross, so that it is fully paying its interest; but there is a debt of 1,000,000*l.* upon it, owing to its having for many years not paid its interest. With the experience we have now had in such works, the project could certainly have been executed for 1,000,000*l.*, and it would have been yielding 15 or 20 per cent. for many years. As it is, I have no doubt it will pay off its debt entirely. The benefits to the people have already been incalculable, having greatly helped that tract of country through a famine, and it will be an inestimable help this year.

"*The Baree Dooab Works.*—I have not the particulars of these works, but I believe they are in a fair way of paying their interest to the Treasury, and they, like all the others, make an enormous return in increase of produce.

"These are the principal new works. There are many others, particularly in the Bombay Presidency, but smaller than these. Thus, notwithstanding the delay in using the water in two of these great works, the actual present return into the Treasury upon the whole expenditure, is certainly 12 or 15 per cent., and the actual benefits may be fairly stated at an average increase of produce of

2*l.* per acre, and an average cost of 2*l.* 10*s.*, or 80 per cent., besides cheap transit."

Sir Arthur then enumerates many valuable works which have for a time been postponed or suspended, and adds:—

"We may safely conclude that there is not one of them that will not cause the loss of tens of thousands of lives, for it is entirely beyond hope that, if the scarcity affects ten or fifteen millions of people, many hundred thousands will not perish, notwithstanding any possible efforts that may be made.

"Had these lines of communication been completed, the upper Godavery country, the upper Mahanuddee, Orissa, the North-West, the Madras provinces, &c., would have been pouring in supplies into the afflicted districts, and immense tracts that will be adding to the general distress would have been, like the Madras districts, not only in perfect plenty, but have been sending vast surplus supplies to those districts.

"Is it possible that a man can still be found who will not heartily help forward the completion of all these works, taking advantage of the multitude of labourers that such a time will place at the disposal of Government?

"I conclude with this one fact—the produce of an acre of rice, 1200 lbs., at the famine price of 1½*d.*, would be 75 rupees, nearly twice the whole *cost of the most expensive of these works, and eight times that of the cheapest*, leaving out the question of life and death to both man and cattle.

"A. COTTON."

APPENDIX C.

EDUCATION OF AGRICULTURAL CLASSES.

COLONEL DAVIDSON'S plan,* as originally proposed by him in May 1839, involved:—

I. To reserve, at each periodical settlement of the land tax, a percentage of the Imperial land revenue for schools, to which a percentage for roads was afterwards added. The reservation to be one anna ($\frac{1}{16}$) in each rupee of Government Assessment equal to 6·18 per cent.

II. To put English and vernacular schools within an accessible distance of each cultivator.

III. To open industrial schools, with factories for the manufacture of carts and agricultural implements attached to them.

IV. To give rewards to enterprising husbandmen, for improved crops, cattle, &c.

He proposed that out of every 2000*l.* so raised, Government should pay 1 European superintendent at 420*l.* per annum, 1 head master at 210*l.* per annum, 3 native examiners at from 30*l.* to 50*l.* per annum, 60 village schools costing from 10*l.* to 25*l.* each per annum, and a central or normal school empowered to grant 10 small

* 'Proposed Scheme for the Education of the Agricultural Classes in Western India.' By Major Davidson. Edinburgh: John Greig and Son. 1873.

scholarships to cost in all about 150*l.* per annum. He insisted on the necessity of a well-educated European superintendent, but the rest of the agency was to be native; and he calculated that it would require nearly double the number of schools he proposed to bring education within two miles of each village. But he preferred the smaller number of good schools, and calculated that he would have about eighty scholars in each school.

At the market-town of the district he proposed to place a few instructed artificers to teach the making of cheap and good carts, and generally to improve the mechanical resources of the district. Any surplus of funds was to be devoted to improving the agriculture of the district. In the central workshop the sons of the village carpenters and blacksmiths round about were to serve a kind of apprenticeship, receiving a small sum from the educational fund to meet their extra expense while so employed, and while attending the adjoining school.

This plan was very gradually adopted, first by Mr. Inverarity, and then on a much more extended scale chiefly through the influence of Mr. Barrow Ellis, in Sind, and ultimately, with the active aid of Sir Alexander Grant, when he was Director-General of Public Instruction, throughout the Bombay Presidency.

In a late note on State Education in India Mr. Howell, Under-Secretary to Government, writes thus of it:—

"*Extracts from Note on State Education in India by* A. P. Howell, Esq., *Under-Secretary to Government of India.*"

"*Par.* 20.—In Dec., 1863, the Bombay Government submitted proposals, which had been under discussion since 1839, for raising funds for the establishment of village schools, and the construction of roads, bridges, &c., in the several districts of that presidency. It was proposed to levy a cess of one anna on every rupee of land revenue (6·18 per cent.), and a tax on wheeled vehicles; the latter part was dropped, and the one anna on each rupee on land revenue sanctioned, and is the source of the Bombay educational cess, which, pending the long discussion to which the measure has given rise, the Bombay Government has continued to levy since 1863-4. Of this anna, one-third goes to education, and two-thirds to roads and works of public utility."

"*Par.* 98.—But by far the most successful feature in the connection of the State with education in this (Bombay) presidency is the establishment and progress of the educational cess, a full account of which I have given above. The cess bids fair to solve the great problem of the despatch of 1854—education for the masses; and it is owing to this cess that the statistics of education in Bombay, when tried by the standard of the educational code, will not be found wanting except in the two points of female education and the development of the grant-in-aid principle, to both of which the attention of the educational authorities during the current year has been specially directed."

A recent report on Colonel Davidson's four propositions states, as regards Proposal I., that an anna in the rupee of assessment is levied for Local Funds, which are administered by a Local Fund Committee, and legalised by Act III., 1869. The scheme of a Local Fund has proved the greatest possible success and benefit to the ryot. But of this anna in the rupee, or an equivalent of one-sixteenth part of the land revenue, one-third goes to form the Educational Fund. It is compulsory throughout British districts in the Bombay Presidency, and yields about 80,000*l.*, with a prospect of increase as the settlements fall in. An imperial grant from the general revenue of about 100,000*l.* is also made (chiefly for high schools and colleges); and as the Government of India do not seem likely to increase that grant, local funds must meet the increasing demand for education.

This, however, cannot be done without taking a larger percentage from the revenue. The problem for the future is, how to meet the increasing demand for education, if, first, the imperial grant is not increased, and, secondly, if the local funds do not expand. The Bombay Government wishes that municipalities should bear their share. These local funds have nothing in common with the recent system of what is called provincial taxation, though the two are often confounded by critics on Indian affairs.

With regard to Colonel Davidson's Proposal II., "To put English and vernacular schools reasonably near each villager's door," it is observed that this hinges on Proposal I. Without more funds there can be no great increase in the number of schools. But a great deal has been done in Western India, perhaps as much as the country at present calls for. The boys are wanted in the fields, and won't stay at school. The number of Government and aided schools in the Bombay presidency is over 4,000, with more than 220,000 pupils. Of these, no less than 180,000 are in primary village schools, and 90,000 are sons of the cess payers, i.e., ryots pure and simple.

With regard to Proposal III., for industrial schools, little has yet been done. The cart-factory, started at Mohol, has long since supplied the whole country round Poona with cheap and good carts. Railways and their workshops have done much to improve the village blacksmiths and carpenters; but much remains to be done in this direction.

Proposal IV. is "To reward enterprising husbandmen."

Here again much remains to be done; but the subject has not been neglected, and agricultural shows and experimental farms have not been without good result. The local officers have been stirred up to encourage an interest in good farming and breeding of cattle; but much more is required before Colonel Davidson's projects of thirty years ago are realised as regards the great mass of the agricultural population.

APPENDIX D.

PROHIBITION OF EXPORTS.

THERE are but two important parts of the policy lately adopted by the Government of India which have not hitherto received from critics in this country the full support and approval they seem to me to deserve. These are the attention devoted to relief works, and the refusal to prohibit the export of grain.

As regards relief works, there can be little doubt, when the full details of the measures authorized by the Government of India are before the public, it will be seen that none of the usual objections to famine relief works can be urged against those which have been undertaken. They are all, so far as the details are yet before us, works of acknowledged permanent value, carefully designed, and carefully estimated for, long previous to any apprehension of famine. The only effect of their being now adopted as famine relief works will be greatly to add to the amount of work for wages which will be provided, at a season when such work would otherwise be most scanty, and to enable Government to pay for such work, either in money or grain in the manner and at the place most convenient for insuring a careful distribution both of work and wages. They will all add greatly to the permanent resources of the country in future years, and tend to protect it against a recurrence of famine whilst they will support, without loss of habit of labour or of self-respect, a vast multitude of the labouring class who would otherwise starve. It may safely be predicted that the action of the Viceroy in ordering such works will be entirely approved, as soon as the details of the measures he has adopted are generally known.

The refusal to prohibit the export of grain has met with more general unfavourable criticism. Those who advocate such a prohibition most strenuously admit that it would be unsound policy in Europe. But we are told that the case of India is so different that it forms an exception to the general rules applicable in such cases.

Dr. Hunter's work on "Famine Warnings" has been quoted to shew that a rise of prices, which will starve Bengal, will not stop exports from Bengal to other countries; and the experience of the last few weeks has been appealed to, as shewing that more rice has been exported from Bengal than has been imported. Hence the inference is drawn that it would have been sound policy to prohibit export, as soon as the famine appeared imminent.

Let us examine how far this inference is sound. First, let us see what is the exact measure recommended, and then what must be its effect.

It is obvious that such a prohibition, to be of any use whatever, ought to have been suddenly issued early in the season, as soon as alarm was felt; otherwise much rice would have left the country before the prohibition could operate.

For like reasons the prohibition must have been indiscriminating as to different kinds of rice; it must have been applicable to the finest, which was not used by the poor peasant in Bengal, but the sale of which to England helped materially to pay his rent, and to support his family, as well as to that coarser rice which is the usual food of the poor in Bengal. Any attempt at discrimination in such an article as rice could only have been a facility for evading the prohibition to export.

For the same reasons the prohibition must have been

indiscriminating as to locality. It must have embraced all India, otherwise export would still have taken place from unusual ports, and by roundabout routes.

Nothing, in short, would have been effectual but such a measure of prohibition as would have given to Government, for the use of the distressed districts of Bengal, the absolute command of all the rice in India.

Let us now first observe that this is not at all what the advocates for the prohibition of exports, writing in Bengal, desire and ask for. One of the main reasons urged by the advocates of the prohibition is that "it would satisfy native opinion—that it would have a good moral effect on the population."

Now, as for its "satisfying native opinion," we must observe that what "native opinion" asks is not simply that export from Bengal should be prohibited, but that surplus rice should everywhere be impounded and locked up, for the benefit of the local consumers. The Bengali newspapers are full of complaints from the eastern districts, where the harvest has been abundant, that *their* rice is being exported to other parts of Bengal. It is not merely the export to Europe that troubles them, but the abstraction of the grain, its being carried away, and becoming more dear to that class of the local population, whose voice alone is heard in the newspapers.

The zemindars of Eastern Bengal are doubtless well content, and so are the cultivators, to get the best price the market affords for their surplus rice; but all the non-cultivating and non-landholding classes—that is, all the well-educated classes whose voice alone can be heard in the native public press in Bengal—naturally exclaim against anything which, by rendering rice dear in Chitagong and Dacca, straitens them. But clearly they would be no better off, if Government seized upon all the rice, and took it for the use of the starving districts, which is virtually what the prohibition of export comes to. For, as regards the starving districts, unless Government took the rice, of which the export was prohibited, and sent it by Government agency to the districts where crops had failed, the rice which is now being exported from Bengal would still be in the wrong place; it would be at Chitagong or Dacca, instead of at Tirhoot or Bagulpore; and "native public opinion," as far as it can be ascertained from correspondents and the native press, would be as strongly expressed against any attempt of Government to take Eastern Bengal rice for the use of the famine-stricken districts in North-Western Bengal, as if the rice were taken for export to London. Government by paying highly might content the landowner, the cultivator, and perhaps even the grain merchant; but the educated class, who in Eastern Bengal are generally men on salaries or with fixed incomes, would still see their neighbour's surplus grain going away and their own food rising in price, and would still naturally complain. The prohibition of export, in fact, must always be a great measure of confiscation; and, however willing Government may be to compensate, it will always be doubtful whether more are not pinched or starved, than fed, by such interference, and the only "native opinion" which can make itself heard will condemn the measure, when its results are realised, as strongly as it advocated it before.

Let us note that the case is not that of a beleaguered city. In the city the whole case is within the grasp of one intellect. Even when Paris was besieged there was power of foreseeing the utmost possible duration of the siege, and the stocks of food, actual and possible, were, within certain limits, capable of calculation, and the careful distribution was within human power to control. But this is not the case with a province, still less with a collection of provinces like Bengal; and, whilst any one road of import remained open, it would have been madness in the commandant of the beleaguered city to do anything to make the grain dealers believe that the Government would supersede their function, or interfere with their profits, as holders and distributors of the grain stocks.

As for any "moral effect" which the prohibition would have, it would probably be of the most disastrous kind. It would discourage import by land as well as by sea, and increase the impression that Government was going to do everything, and that the population itself might fold its hands and await events.

The refusal to prohibit export is generally treated by the English press as a doctrinaire notion, which could be entertained by none but political economists, who cared for nothing but their theory. But the fact is, the measure has been condemned by all the most experienced practical men, who have ever had anything on a great scale, to do with famines.

There are probably no two better practical Indian authorities who have written on the subject, after long observation of our worst famines, than the late Colonel Baird Smith, in his "Report on the Great North-Western Famine," printed as a Parliamentary Blue Book, in 1862, and Sir Geo. Campbell, in his "Report on the Orissa Famine," printed in 1867. Both these valuable works are full of the most overwhelming evidence, to show how dangerous in any great famine is such a measure as the prohibition of the export of grain, or any interference with its transit, except in the way of affording every facility for it to go wherever it naturally is inclined to go. I cannot believe that the Lieutenant-Governor of Bengal has so far forgotten the teachings of his own invaluable "Report on Orissa" as to advocate nakedly the prohibition of export. I have no doubt, when all the correspondence on the subject is laid before the public, it will be found that what he really advocated was, not so much a prohibition of export as its discouragement by purchase—a measure of a totally different character. However that may be, I think any one calmly reading his remarks on Orissa, on the infinite importance of encouraging to the utmost the natural grain trade, not merely as a source of supply, but as a means of natural circulation and distribution of the food, will conclude, with the Government of India, that no more disastrous step could have been taken than to have prohibited exportation.

We have now some means of judging what would have been the effect had such a measure been adopted in November. The latest telegrams inform us that 90,000 tons of food have already been exported from Bengal by sea. No mention is made of how much of this rice was of the kind usually consumed by the poor, and how much of the kind they habitually export, to be sold at higher prices than their own food-rice, and to help to buy coarser rice, and to pay for rent, clothes, &c.; but supposing it to have been all of the coarsest kind, what would have been the effect of impounding it? The latest estimates of the numbers which may need help in getting food during the coming months do not differ materially from the estimates formerly framed. We are told that there will be, in a distressed population of twenty-five millions, something like two and a half millions of people who will be unable entirely to feed themselves, for periods varying from four to eight months. Let us see what the 90,000 tons of food would have done for them, if impounded and distributed by Government. It would have fed two and a half millions of starving or half-starving people at the rate of 1 lb. per diem for only eighty days. There would have been little to spare for the other twenty-two and a half millions of hard-pressed people; and, looking to the enormous difficulties of Government distribution, it may safely be said that no such task could have been accomplished by any but the natural agency of grain dealers and zemindars.

It may be said that this 90,000 tons of food is not the whole amount likely to be exported. I find, from the best references accessible, that during the last twenty years the annual export of rice from Bengal has varied from nil to 900,000 tons. The average seems to be between 400,000 and 500,000 tons since 1855—56, which appears to be the first year of great export. But this quantity could only be exported in a year of average produce; and there can be little doubt that, even if Government had impounded every ton of this year's surplus grain, the whole quantity would have been insufficient to meet the demand caused by any attempt on the part of the Government to supercede the trader in distributing grain and feeding the people.

But at what cost would the attempt have been made? As soon as it was known that Government intended to adopt such a measure, all but the most pedling trade would have been at once paralysed. None but a gambling speculator, calculating on the breakdown of the Government, would have ventured to deal in such a hazardous article as grain. However tempting the prospect, all cautious merchants would have abstained from an article of trade regarding which Government had emphatically declared, by its acts, that it would consider nothing but its own view of the wants of the consumer. Government, when it once enters on such a course, must reserve to itself the right to confiscate or not to confiscate—to distribute or not to distribute, all stocks of food. It must necessarily, also, reserve to itself the right to judge of the price to be given; and no man in his senses would trust his capital in such a venture as a grain speculation, the profits of which were to depend on the will of the Government. The measure must have broken down, and ended in disastrous failure, as soon as the real strain of famine began to tell; and no power on earth could have managed such a task as the commissariat of two and a half millions of ignorant starving men dispersed over the country.

Something might have been said for such a measure had Bengal contained sufficient supply of food for the whole population, and had it been possible that a simple prohibition of export would have left the trade free to move the grain about as it was wanted. But we all know that neither postulate can be granted. The grain does not exist in Bengal. It must be brought from without; and much has come in, from other parts of India, which certainly would not have come had export been prohibited, and the trader been alarmed. It may be true that no importer save Government has yet gone to the markets of Burmah, the Eastern Islands, China, or Saigoon; but it is quite possible that large stocks can yet be imported from all these quarters; and if they are not imported, the importation would certainly not be promoted by a prohibition of export. It may be necessary for Government to purchase on the spot, or to offer bounties on import, or to resort to other measures which may help the natural operation of famine prices; but a prohibition of export could only counteract that natural action, and, so far as it did so, would intensify the sufferings from famine.

The following useful tables have been drawn up by Mr. Trelawney Saunders, to illustrate his Maps:—

A LIST OF THE TOWNS

WITH A POPULATION EXCEEDING FIVE THOUSAND IN THE DISTRICTS THREATENED WITH FAMINE.

PATNA DIVISION.

District Patna—

	Population.
Patna	158,900
Behar	44,295
Dinapore Nizamut	27,914
" Cantonment	14,170
Futuha	11,295
Barh	11,050
Mokameh	10,715
Muhammadpore	6,089
Baikatpore	6,088
Muneer	5,326
Khagowl	5,257

District Gyah—

	Population.
Gyah	66,843
Jehanabad	21,022
Daoodnuggur	10,058
Tikaree	8,178
Sherghotty	7,033
Hisooah	6,119
Rajowlee	5,012

District Shahabad—

	Population.
Arrah	39,386
Sasseram	21,023
Doomraon	17,356
Buxar	13,466
Jugdeespore	9,400
Bhojpore	7,004
Nasrigunje	5,732
Bhubhooa	5,071

District Tirhoot—

	Population.
Durbhangah	47,450
Mozufferpore	38,223
Hajeepore	22,306
Lalgunje	12,338
Rowserah	9,441
Seetamurhee	5,496

District Sarun—

	Population.
Chupra	46,287
Revilgunje	13,415
Sewan	11,099

District Chumparun—

	Population.
Bettiah	19,708
Moteeharee	8,266

BHAUGULPORE DIVISION.

District Bhaugulpore.

	Population.
Bhaugulpore	69,673
Colgong	5,239

District Monghyr—

	Population.
Monghyr	59,693
Shaikpoorah	11,536
Jumalpore	10,453
Burheea	10,405
Soorajghurrah	7,935
Barbigha	6,362
Jumoee	5,197

District Purneah—

	Population.
Purneah	16,057
Raneegunje	6,144

BURDWAN DIVISION.

	POPULATION.
District Bancoorah—	
Bishenpore	18,047
Bancoorah	16,794
District Beerbhoom—	
Soory	9,001
District Burdwan—	
Burdwan	32,321
Culnah	27,336
Shambazar	19,635
Raneegunje	19,578
Jehanabad	13,409
Cutwa	7,963
Dain Hat	7,562
District Hoogly and Howrah—	
Hoogly and Howrah	97,784
Chinsurah	34,761
Serampore	24,440
Buddybatee	13,332
Bansbarea	7,861
Bhudressur	7,417
Kotrung	6,811
District Midnapore—	
Midnapore	31,491
Chundrakona	21,311
Ghatal	15,492
Tumlook	5,849

RAJSHAYE DIVISION.

	POPULATION.
District Moorshedabad—	
City Moorshedabad	46,182
Berhampore	27,110
Kandy	12,016
Junghypore	11,361
Beldanga	6,037
Morgram	5,766
District Dinajpore—	
Dinajpore	13,042
District Maldah—	
English Bazaar	12,859
Maldah	5,262
District Rajshaye—	
Rampore Bauliah	22,291
Nattore	9,674
District Rungpore—	
Rungpore	14,845
District Pubnah—	
Serajgunje	18,873
Pubnah	15,730
Belkuchee	5,128
District Bograh—	
Bograh	5,872

A TABLE OF THE AREA AND POPULATION OF THE DIVISIONS AND DISTRICTS THREATENED WITH FAMINE IN 1874.

Population per square mile.	Divisions and Districts.	Executive sub-divisions.	Area in square miles.	Population.	District Chief Town and Population.		Number of Towns and Villages.
	LOWER PROVINCES.						
	Patna Division—						
413	District Gyah (Behar) ..	4	4,718	1,949,750	Gyah	66,843	6,530
742	„ Patna	4	2,101	1,559,638	Patna	158,900	3,412
778	„ Sarun	2	2,654	2,063,860	Chupra	46,287	4,350
408	„ Chumparun ..	2	3,531	1,440,815	Moteeharee ..	8,266	2,299
393	„ Shahabad	4	4,385	1,723,974	Arrah	39,386	5,110
691	„ Tirhoot	6	6,343	4,384,706	Mozufferpore ..	38,223	7,337
			23,732	13,122,743			29,038
	Bhaugulpore Division—						
422	District Bhaugulpore ..	4	4,327	1,826,290	Bhaugulpore ..	69,678	2,739
463	„ Monghyr	3	3,913	1,812,986	Monghyr	59,698	2,457
346	„ Purneah	3	4,957	1,714,795	Purneah	16,057	4,179
229	„ Sonthal Purgunnahs	4	5,488	1,259,287	—	—	9,872
			18,685	6,613,358			19,247

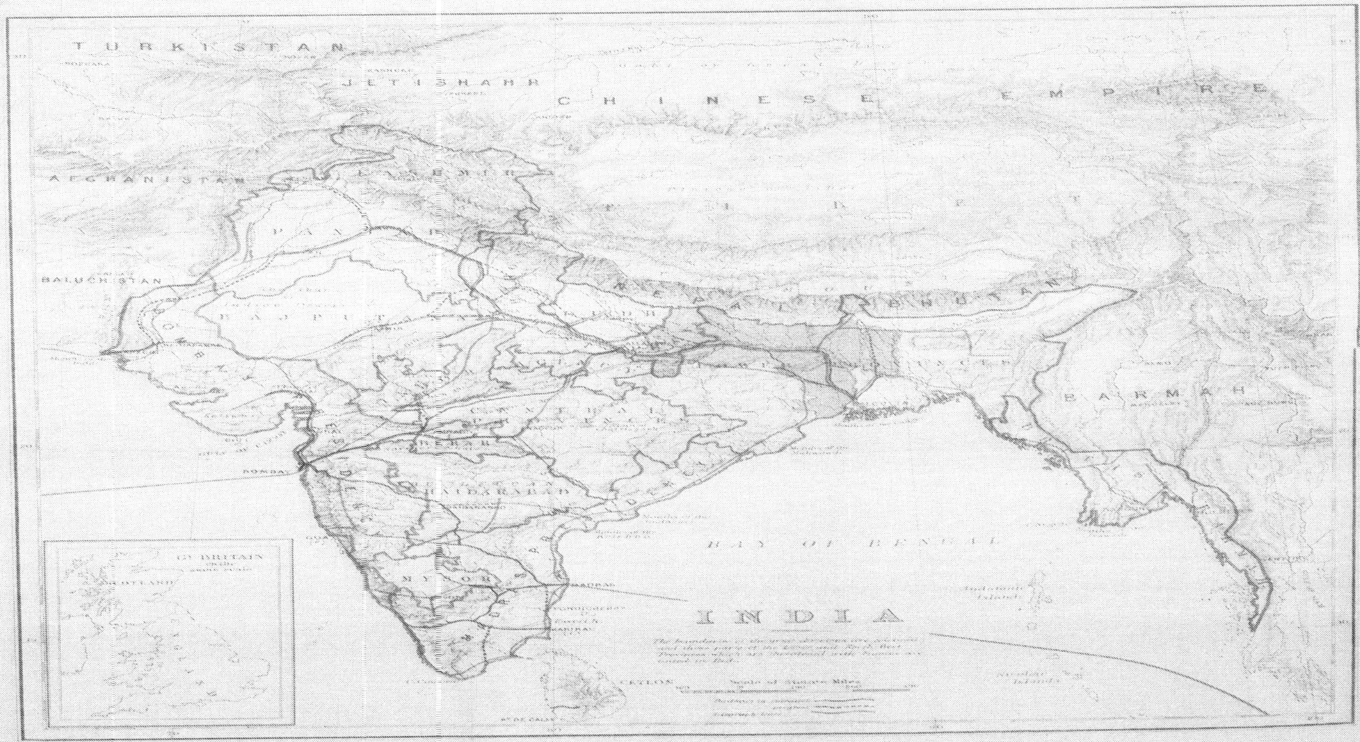
TURKISTAN
JETISHAHR
CHINESE EMPIRE
AFGHANISTAN
BALUCHISTAN
BHUTAN
BARMAH
BOMBAY
BAY OF BENGAL
CEYLON
G^t BRITAIN
SCOTLAND
INDIA
Scale of Statute Miles

	Rajshaye Division—						
459	District Bograh	1	1,501	689,467	Bograh	5,872	2,666
364	„ Dinajpore	1	4,126	1,501,924	Dinajpore	13,042	7,108
373	„ Maldah	1	1,813	676,426	English Bazaar ..	12,859	2,100
525	„ Moorshedabad ..	4	2,578	1,353,626	Berhampore ..	27,110	3,753
616	„ Pubnah	2	1,966	1,211,594	Pubnah	15,730	2,792
587	„ Rajshaye	2	2,234	1,310,729	Rampore Bauliah	22,291	4,228
619	„ Rungpore	2	3,476	2,149,972	Rungpore	14,845	4,206
			17,694	8,893,738			26,853
	Burdwan Division—						
391	District Bancoorah	1	1,346	526,772	Bancoorah ..	16,984	2,028
518	„ Beerbhoom	1	1,344	695,921	Soory	9,001	2,471
578	„ Burdwan	6	3,523	2,034,745	Burdwan	32,321	5,191
1,045	„ Hoogly with Howrah	3	1,424	1,488,556	Hoogly	34,761	3,190
500	„ Midnapore	4	5,082	2,540,963	Midnapore ..	31,491	12,962
			12,719	7,286,957			25,842
	NORTH-WEST PROVINCES.						
	Benares Division—						
	District Azimgurh	6	2,550	1,497,580	Azimgurh ..	14,543	6,316
	„ Benares	2	995	793,433	Benares	172,352	2,299
	„ Ghazeepore ..	6	2,226	1,454,000	Ghazeepore ..	34,385	5,115
	„ Ghoruckpore ..	6	4,585	2,044,821	Ghoruckpore ..	50,853	8,361
	„ Mirzapore	3	5,200	1,087,200	Mirzapore ..	71,849	5,376
			15,556	6,877,034			27,467

SUMMARY.

Rate of Population per sq. mile.		Area in in square miles.	Population.	Number of Towns and Villages.
269	The Lower Provinces	248,231	66,856,859	200,938
	THREATENED DIVISIONS *in the Lower Provinces.*			
553	Patna Division	23,732	13,122,743	29,038
354	Bhaugulpore Division	18,685	6,613,358	19,247
503	Rajshaye Division	17,694	8,893,738	26,853
573	Burdwan Division	12,719	7,286,957	25,842
	THREATENED DIVISION *in the North-West Provinces.*			
442	Benares Division	15,556	6,877,034	27,467
	Threatened Totals ..	88,386	42,793,830	128,446

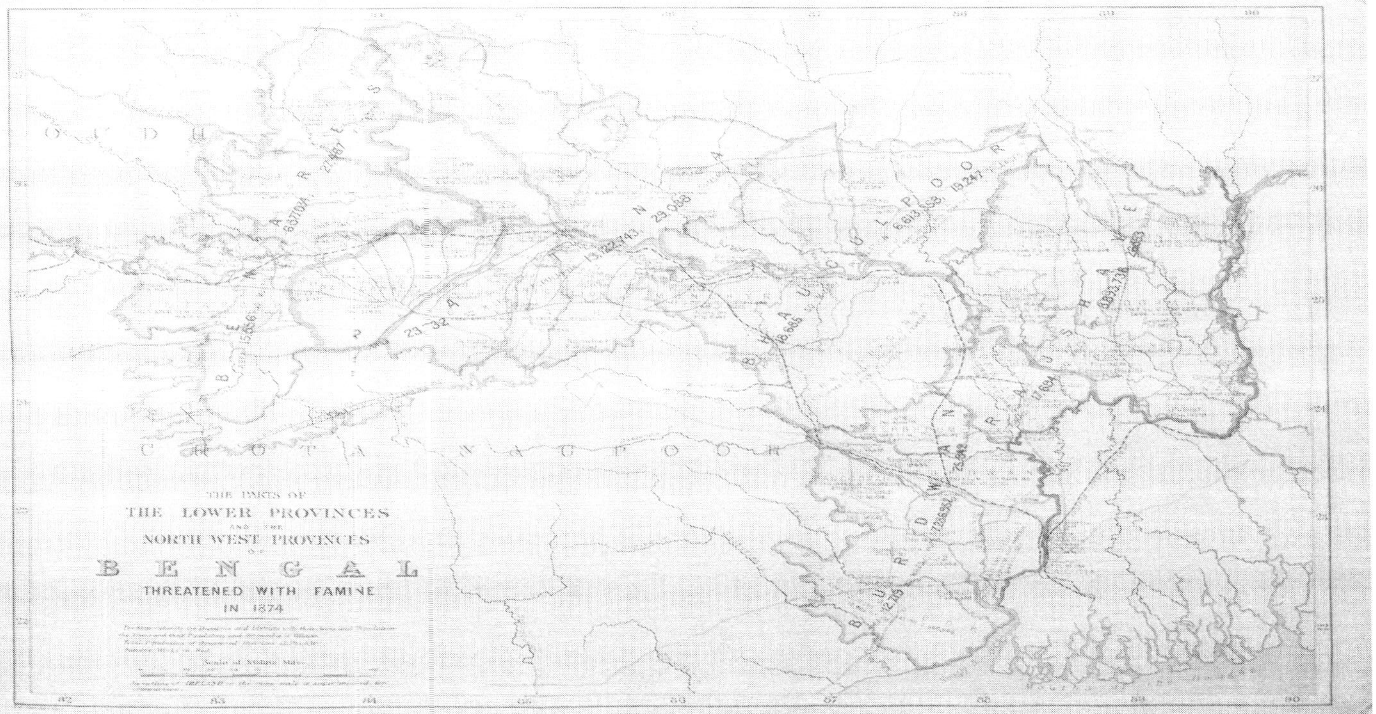
THE PARTS OF
THE LOWER PROVINCES
AND THE
NORTH WEST PROVINCES
OF
B E N G A L
THREATENED WITH FAMINE
IN 1874
O U D H
C H O T A N A G P O O R

ALBEMARLE STREET, LONDON,
February, 1873.

MR. MURRAY'S

GENERAL LIST OF WORKS.

ALBERT (THE) MEMORIAL. The National Monument erected to the PRINCE CONSORT at Kensington. Illustrated by Engravings of its Architecture, Decorations; Sculptured Groups, Statues, Mosaics, Metalwork, &c. With Descriptive Text. With 24 Plates. Folio. 12*l*. 12*s*. Large Paper. 15*l*. 15*s*. Published by Authority.

*** A POPULAR HANDBOOK to the above Monument. Woodcuts. 16mo. 1*s*.

——— (PRINCE) SPEECHES AND ADDRESSES ON PUBLIC Occasions; with an Introduction, giving some outline of his Character. With Portrait. 8vo. 10*s*. 6*d*.; or *Popular Edition*, fcap. 8vo. 1*s*.

ABBOTT'S (REV. J.) Memoirs of a Church of England Missionary in the North American Colonies. Post 8vo. 2*s*.

ABERCROMBIE'S (JOHN) Enquiries concerning the Intellectual Powers and the Investigation of Truth. 19*th Edition*. Fcap. 8vo. 3*s*. 6*d*.

——— Philosophy of the Moral Feelings. 14*th Edition*. Fcap. 8vo. 2*s*. 6*d*.

ACLAND'S (REV. CHARLES) Popular Account of the Manners and Customs of India. Post 8vo. 2*s*.

ÆSOP'S FABLES. A New Version. With Historical Preface. By Rev. THOMAS JAMES. With 100 Woodcuts, by TENNIEL and WOLF. 64*th Thousand*. Post 8vo. 2*s*. 6*d*.

AGRICULTURAL (ROYAL) JOURNAL. 8vo. 6*s*. (*Half yearly.*)

AIDS TO FAITH: a Series of Theological Essays. 8vo. 9*s*.

CONTENTS.

Miracles	DEAN MANSEL.
Evidences of Christianity	BISHOP OF KILLALOE.
Prophecy & Mosaic Record of Creation	REV. DR MCCAUL.
Ideology and Subscription	CANON COOK.
The Pentateuch	CANON RAWLINSON.
Inspiration	BISHOP OF ELY.
Death of Christ	ARCHBISHOP OF YORK.
Scripture and its Interpretation	BISHOP OF GLOUCESTER AND BRISTOL.

AMBER-WITCH (THE). A most interesting Trial for Witchcraft. Translated by LADY DUFF GORDON. Post 8vo. 2*s*.

ARMY LIST (THE). *Published Monthly by Authority*. 18mo. 2*s*.

ARTHUR'S (LITTLE) History of England. By LADY CALLCOTT. *New Edition, continued to* 1872. Woodcuts. Fcap. 8vo. 2*s*. 6*d*.

AUSTIN'S (JOHN) LECTURES ON GENERAL JURISPRUDENCE; or, the Philosophy of Positive Law. 5*th Edition*. Edited by ROBERT CAMPBELL. 2 Vols. 8vo. 32*s*.

——— (SARAH) Fragments from German Prose Writers. With Biographical Notes. Post 8vo. 10*s*.

ADMIRALTY PUBLICATIONS; Issued by direction of the Lords Commissioners of the Admiralty:—

A MANUAL OF SCIENTIFIC ENQUIRY, for the Use of Travellers. Edited by Sir JOHN F. HERSCHEL and ROBERT MAIN, M.A. *Fourth Edition.* Woodcuts. Post 8vo. 3*s*. 6*d*.

AIRY'S ASTRONOMICAL OBSERVATIONS MADE AT GREENWICH. 1836 to 1847. Royal 4to. 50*s*. each.

——— MAGNETICAL AND METEOROLOGICAL OBSERVATIONS. 1840 to 1847. Royal 4to. 50*s*. each.

——— ASTRONOMICAL, MAGNETICAL, AND METEOROLOGICAL OBSERVATIONS, 1848 to 1870. Royal 4to. 50*s*. each.

——— APPENDICES TO THE ASTRONOMICAL OBSERVATIONS.

1836.—I. Bessel's Refraction Tables.
II. Tables for converting Errors of R.A. and N.P.D. into Errors of Longitude and Ecliptic P.D. } 8*s*.

1837.—I. Logarithms of Sines and Cosines to every Ten Seconds of Time.
II. Table for converting Sidereal into Mean Solar Time. } 8*s*.

1842.—Catalogue of 1439 Stars. 8*s*.

1845.—Longitude of Valentia. 8*s*.

1847.—Description of Altazimuth. (*Reprint.*) 5*s*.

1851.—Maskelyne's Ledger of Stars. 6*s*.

1852.—I. Description of the Transit Circle. (*Reprint.*) 5*s*.
II. Regulations of the Royal Observatory. 2*s*.

1853.—Bessel's Refraction Tables. 3*s*.

1854.—I. Description of the Zenith Tube. 3*s*.
II. Six Years' Catalogue of Stars. 10*s*.

1856.—Description of the Galvanic Apparatus at Greenwich Observatory. 8*s*.

1862.—I. Seven Years' Catalogue of Stars. 10*s*.
II. Plan of the Building and Ground of the Royal Observatory, Greenwich.
III. Longitude of Valentia. } 3*s*.

1864.—I. Moon's Semidiameter.
II. Planetary Observations, 1831 to 1835.

1868.—I. Corrections of Bouvard's Elements of Jupiter and Saturn. 4*s*.
II. Seven Years' Catalogue of 2760 Stars for 1864. 10*s*.
III. Description of the Great Equatoreal. 5*s*.

——— ASTRONOMICAL RESULTS. 1848 to 1870. 4to. 8*s*.

——— MAGNETICAL AND METEOROLOGICAL RESULTS. 1848 to 1870. 4to. 8*s*. each.

——— REDUCTION OF THE OBSERVATIONS OF PLANETS. 1750 to 1830. Royal 4to. 50*s*.

——————— LUNAR OBSERVATIONS. 1750 to 1830. 2 Vols. Royal 4to. 50*s*. each.

——————— 1831 to 1851. 4to. 20*s*.

BERNOULLI'S SEXCENTENARY TABLE. *London*, 1779. 4to. 5*s*.

BESSEL'S AUXILIARY TABLES FOR HIS METHOD OF CLEARING LUNAR DISTANCES. 8vo. 2*s*.

ADMIRALTY PUBLICATIONS—*continued.*

COOK, KING, AND BAYLY'S ASTRONOMICAL OBSERVATIONS. *London*, 1782. 4to. 21*s.*

ENCKE'S BERLINER JAHRBUCH, for 1830. *Berlin*, 1828. 8vo 9*s.*

HANSEN'S TABLES DE LA LUNE. 4to. 20*s.*

HARRISON'S PRINCIPLES OF HIS TIME-KEEPER. PLATES. 1797. 4to. 5*s.*

LAX'S TABLES FOR FINDING THE LATITUDE AND LONGITUDE. 1821. 8vo. 10*s.*

LUNAR OBSERVATIONS at GREENWICH. 1783 to 1819. Compared with the Tables, 1821. 4to. 7*s.* 6*d.*

MACLEAR ON LACAILLE'S ARC OF MERIDIAN. 2 Vols. 20*s.*

MASKELYNE'S ACCOUNT OF THE GOING OF HARRISON'S WATCH. 1767. 4to. 2*s.* 6*d.*

MAYER'S DISTANCES of the MOON'S CENTRE from the PLANETS. 1822, 3*s.*; 1823, 4*s.* 6*d.* 1824 to 1835. 8vo. 4*s.* each.

——— TABULÆ MOTUUM SOLIS ET LUNÆ. 1770. 5*s.*

——— ASTRONOMICAL OBSERVATIONS MADE AT GOTTINGEN, from 1756 to 1761. 1826. Folio. 7*s.* 6*d.*

NAUTICAL ALMANACS, from 1767 to 1876. 8vo. 2*s.* 6*d.* each.

——— SELECTIONS FROM THE ADDITIONS up to 1812. 8vo. 5*s.* 1834-54. 8vo. 5*s.*

——— SUPPLEMENTS, 1828 to 1833, 1837 and 1838. 8vo. 2*s.* each.

——— TABLE requisite to be used with the N.A. 1781. 8vo. 5*s.*

POND'S ASTRONOMICAL OBSERVATIONS. 1811 to 1835. 4to. 21*s.* each.

SABINE'S PENDULUM EXPERIMENTS to DETERMINE THE FIGURE OF THE EARTH. 1825. 4to. 40*s.*

SHEPHERD'S TABLES for CORRECTING LUNAR DISTANCES. 1772. Royal 4to. 21*s.*

——— TABLES, GENERAL, of the MOON'S DISTANCE from the SUN, and 10 STARS. 1787. Folio. 5*s.* 6*d.*

TAYLOR'S SEXAGESIMAL TABLE. 1780. 4to. 15*s.*

——— TABLES OF LOGARITHMS. 4to. 3*l.*

TIARK'S ASTRONOMICAL OBSERVATIONS for the LONGITUDE of MADEIRA. 1822. 4to. 5*s.*

——— CHRONOMETRICAL OBSERVATIONS for DIFFERENCES of LONGITUDE between DOVER, PORTSMOUTH, and FALMOUTH. 1823. 4to. 5*s.*

VENUS and JUPITER: OBSERVATIONS of, compared with the TABLES. *London*, 1822. 4to. 2*s.*

WALES' AND BAYLY'S ASTRONOMICAL OBSERVATIONS 1777. 4to. 21*s.*

WALES' REDUCTION OF ASTRONOMICAL OBSERVATIONS MADE IN THE SOUTHERN HEMISPHERE. 1764—1771. 1788. 4to 10*s.* 6*d.*

BARBAULD'S (MRS.) Hymns in Prose for Children. With 112 Illustrations. Small 4to. 5*s.*; or *Fine Paper*, 7*s.* 6*d.*

BARROW'S (SIR JOHN) Autobiographical Memoir, from Early Life to Advanced Age. Portrait. 8vo. 16*s.*

——— (JOHN) Life, Exploits, and Voyages of Sir Francis Drake. Post 8vo. 2*s.*

BARRY'S (SIR CHARLES) Life and Works. By CANON BARRY, D.D. *Second Edition.* With Portrait and Illustrations. Medium 8vo. 15s.

BATES' (H. W.) Records of a Naturalist on the River Amazon during eleven years of Adventure and Travel. *Third Edition.* Illustrations. Post 8vo.

BEAUCLERK'S (LADY DIANA) Summer and Winter in Norway. *Third Edition.* With Illustrations. Small 8vo. 6s.

BEES AND FLOWERS. Two Essays. By REV. THOMAS JAMES. Reprinted from the "Quarterly Review." Fcap. 8vo. 1s. each.

BELCHER'S (LADY) Account of the Mutineers of the 'Bounty,' and their Descendants; with their Settlements in Pitcairn and Norfolk Islands. With Illustrations. Post 8vo. 12s.

BELL'S (SIR CHAS.) Familiar Letters. Portrait. Post 8vo. 12s.

BERTRAM'S (JAS. G.) Harvest of the Sea: a Contribution to the Natural and Economic History of British Food Fishes. *Second Edition.* With 50 Illustrations. 8vo. 12s.

BIBLE COMMENTARY. EXPLANATORY and CRITICAL. With a REVISION of the TRANSLATION. By BISHOPS and CLERGY of the ANGLICAN CHURCH. Edited by F. C. COOK, M.A., Canon of Exeter. Medium 8vo. VOL. I. 30s. VOL. II. 20s.

Vol. I.	GENESIS	Bishop of Ely.
	EXODUS	Canon Cook & Rev. Sam. Clark.
	LEVITICUS	Rev. Samuel Clark.
	NUMBERS	Canon Espin & Rev. J. F. Thrupp.
	DEUTERONOMY	Canon Espin.
Vol. II.	JOSHUA	Canon Espin.
	JUDGES, RUTH, SAMUEL	Bishop of Bath and Wells.
	I. KINGS	Canon Rawlinson.

BICKMORE'S (A. S.) Travels in the Eastern Archipelago, 1865-6; a Popular Description of the Islands, with their Natural History, Geography, Manners and Customs of the People, &c. With Maps and Illustrations. 8vo. 21s.

BIRCH'S (SAMUEL) History of Ancient Pottery and Porcelain: Egyptian, Assyrian, Greek, Roman, and Etruscan. *Second Edition.* With 200 Illustrations. Medium 8vo. 42s.

BISSET'S (ANDREW) History of the Commonwealth of England, from the Death of Charles I. to the Expulsion of the Long Parliament by Cromwell. Chiefly from the MSS. in the State Paper Office. 2 vols. 8vo. 30s.

BLUNT'S (REV. J. J.) Undesigned Coincidences in the Writings of the Old and New Testament, an Argument of their Veracity: containing the Books of Moses, Historical and Prophetical Scriptures, and the Gospels and Acts. *Eleventh Edition.* Post 8vo. 6s.

——— History of the Church in the First Three Centuries. *Fifth Edition.* Post 8vo. 6s.

——— Parish Priest; His Duties, Acquirements and Obligations. *Fifth Edition.* Post 8vo. 6s.

——— Lectures on the Right Use of the Early Fathers. *Third Edition.* 8vo. 9s.

——— Plain Sermons Preached to a Country Congregation. *Sixth Edition.* 2 Vols. Post 8vo. 12s.

——— Essays on various subjects. 8vo. 12s.

BLOMFIELD'S (BISHOP) Memoir, with Selections from his Correspondence. By his Son. *Second Edition.* Portrait, post 8vo. 12*s.*

BOSWELL'S (JAMES) Life of Samuel Johnson, LL.D. Including the Tour to the Hebrides. Edited by Mr. CROKER. Portraits. Royal 8vo. 10*s.*

BRACE'S (C. L.) Manual of Ethnology; or the Races of the Old World. Post 8vo. 6*s.*

BOOK OF COMMON PRAYER. Illustrated with Coloured Borders, Initial Letters, and Woodcuts. 8vo. 18*s.*

BORROW'S (GEORGE) Bible in Spain; or the Journeys, Adventures, and Imprisonments of an Englishman in an Attempt to circulate the Scriptures in the Peninsula. Post 8vo. 3*s.* 6*d.*

——— Zincali, or the Gipsies of Spain; their Manners, Customs, Religion, and Language. Post 8vo. 3*s.* 6*d.*

——— Lavengro; The Scholar—The Gipsy—and the Priest. Post 8vo. 5*s.*

——— Romany Rye—a Sequel to "Lavengro." Post 8vo. 5*s.*

——— WILD WALES: its People, Language, and Scenery. Post 8vo. 5*s.*

BRAY'S (MRS.) Life of Thomas Stothard, R.A. With Portrait and 60 Woodcuts. 4to. 21*s.*

——— Revolt of the Protestants in the Cevennes. With some Account of the Huguenots in the Seventeenth Century. Post 8vo. 10*s.* 6*d.*

BRITISH ASSOCIATION REPORTS. 8vo.

York and Oxford, 1831-32, 13*s.* 6*d.*
Cambridge, 1833, 12*s.*
Edinburgh, 1834, 15*s.*
Dublin, 1835, 13*s.* 6*d.*
Bristol, 1836, 12*s.*
Liverpool, 1837, 16*s.* 6*d.*
Newcastle, 1838, 15*s.*
Birmingham, 1839, 13*s.* 6*d*
Glasgow, 1840, 15*s.*
Plymouth, 1841, 13*s.* 6*d.*
Manchester, 1842, 10*s.* 6*d.*
Cork, 1843, 12*s.*
York, 1844, 20*s.*
Cambridge, 1845, 12*s.*
Southampton, 1846, 15*s.*
Oxford, 1847, 18*s.*
Swansea, 1848, 9*s.*
Birmingham, 1849, 10*s.*
Edinburgh, 1850, 15*s.*
Ipswich, 1851, 16*s.* 6*d.*
Belfast, 1852, 15*s.*
Hull, 1853, 10*s.* 6*d.*
Liverpool, 1854, 18*s.*
Glasgow, 1855, 15*s.*
Cheltenham, 1856, 18*s.*
Dublin, 1857, 15*s.*
Leeds, 1858, 20*s.*
Aberdeen, 1859, 15*s.*
Oxford, 1860, 25*s.*
Manchester, 1861, 15*s.*
Cambridge, 1862, 20*s.*
Newcastle, 1863, 25*s.*
Bath, 1864, 18*s.*
Birmingham, 1865, 25*s*
Nottingham, 1866, 24*s.*
Dundee, 1867, 26*s.*
Norwich, 1868, 25*s.*
Exeter, 1869, 22*s.*
Liverpool, 1870, 18*s.*
Edinburgh, 1871, 16*s.*

BROUGHTON'S (LORD) Journey through Albania, Turkey in Europe and Asia, to Constantinople. Illustrations. 2 Vols. 8vo. 30*s.*

——— Visits to Italy. 2 Vols. Post 8vo. 18*s.*

BROWNLOW'S (LADY) Reminiscences of a Septuagenarian. From the year 1802 to 1815. *Third Edition.* Post 8vo. 7*s.* 6*d.*

BUBBLES FROM THE BRUNNEN OF NASSAU. By Sir FRANCIS B. HEAD, Bart. *7th Edition.* Illustrations. Post 8vo. 7*s.* 6*d.*

BUNYAN (JOHN) and Oliver Cromwell. By ROBERT SOUTHEY. Post 8vo. 2*s.*

BURGON'S (REV. J. W.) Christian Gentleman; or, Memoir of Patrick Fraser Tytler. *Second Edition.* Post 8vo. 9*s.*

——— Letters from Rome. Post 8vo. 12*s.*

BURN'S (Col.) Dictionary of Naval and Military Technical Terms, English and French—French and English. *Fourth Edition.* Crown 8vo. 15s.

BURROW'S (Montagu) Constitutional Progress. A Series of Lectures delivered before the University of Oxford. *2nd Edition.* Post 8vo. 5s.

BUXTON'S (Charles) Memoirs of Sir Thomas Fowell Buxton, Bart. With Selections from his Correspondence. Portrait. 8vo. 16s. *Popular Edition.* Fcap. 8vo. 5s.

——— Notes of Thought. With Biographical Sketch. By Rev. Llewellyn Davies. With Portrait. Crown 8vo. 10s. 6d.

——— Ideas of the Day on Policy. *3rd Edition.* 8vo. 6s.

BURCKHARDT'S (Dr. Jacob) Cicerone; or Art Guide to Painting in Italy. Edited by Rev. Dr. A. Von Zahn, and Translated from the German by Mrs. A. Clough. Post 8vo.

BYRON'S (Lord) Letters and Journals. By Thomas Moore. *Cabinet Edition.* Plates. 6 Vols. Fcap. 8vo. 18s.

——— *Popular Edition.* Portraits. Royal 8vo.

——— Poetical Works. *Library Edition.* Portrait. 6 Vols. Demy 8vo. 45s.

——— *Cabinet Edition.* Plates. 10 Vols. Fcap. 8vo. 30s.

——— *Pocket Edition.* 8 Vols. 24mo. 21s. *Bound, and in a Case.*

——— *Popular Edition.* Plates. Royal 8vo.

——— *Pearl Edition.* Crown 8vo. 2s. 6d.

——— Childe Harold. With 80 Engravings. 8vo. 12s.

——— 16mo. 2s. 6d.

——— Vignettes. 16mo. 1s.

——— Portrait. 16mo. 6d.

——— Tales and Poems. 24mo. 2s. 6d.

——— Miscellaneous. 2 Vols. 24mo. 5s.

——— Dramas and Plays. 2 Vols. 24mo. 5s.

——— Don Juan and Beppo. 2 Vols. 24mo. 5s.

——— Beauties. Portrait. Fcap. 8vo. 3s. 6d.

BURR'S (G. D.) Instructions in Practical Surveying, Topographical Plan Drawing, and on sketching ground without Instruments. *Fourth Edition.* Woodcuts. Post 8vo. 6s.

BUTTMAN'S LEXILOGUS; a Critical Examination of the Meaning of numerous Greek Words, chiefly in Homer and Hesiod. Translated by Rev. J. R. Fishlake. *Fifth Edition.* 8vo. 12s.

——— CATALOGUE OF IRREGULAR GREEK VERBS. With all the Tenses extant—their Formation, Meaning, and Usage, accompanied by an Index. Translated, with Notes, by Rev. J. R. Fishlake. *Fifth Edition.* Revised by Rev. E. Venables. Post 8vo. 6s.

CALLCOTT'S (Lady) Little Arthur's History of England. *New Edition, brought down to* 1872. With Woodcuts. Fcap. 8vo. 2s. 6d.

CAMPBELL'S (LORD) Lives of the Lord Chancellors and Keepers of the Great Seal of England. From the Earliest Times to the Death of Lord Eldon in 1838. *Fourth Edition.* 10 Vols. Crown 8vo. 6*s.* each.

———— Lords Lyndhurst and Brougham. 8vo. 16*s.*

———— Chief Justices of England. From the Norman Conquest to the Death of Lord Tenterden. *Second Edition.* 3 Vols. 8vo. 42*s.*

———— Shakspeare's Legal Acquirements. 8vo. 5*s.* 6*d.*

———— Life of Lord Bacon. Fcap. 8vo. 2*s.* 6*d.*

———— (SIR NEIL) Account of Napoleon at Fontainebleau and Elba. Being a Journal of Occurrences and Notes of his Conversations, &c. Portrait. 8vo. 15*s.*

———— (GEORGE) Modern India. A Sketch of the System of Civil Government. With some Account of the Natives and Native Institutions. *Second Edition.* 8vo. 16*s.*

———— (THOS.) Essay on English Poetry. With Short Lives of the British Poets. Post 8vo. 3*s.* 6*d.*

CARNARVON'S (LORD) Portugal, Gallicia, and the Basque Provinces. *Third Edition.* Post 8vo. 3*s.* 6*d.*

———— Reminiscences of Athens and the Morea. With Map. Crown 8vo. 7*s.* 6*d.*

———— Recollections of the Druses of Lebanon. With Notes on their Religion. *Third Edition.* Post 8vo. 5*s.* 6*d.*

CASTLEREAGH (THE) DESPATCHES, from the commencement of the official career of Viscount Castlereagh to the close of his life. 12 Vols. 8vo. 14*s.* each.

CATHCART'S (SIR GEORGE) Commentaries on the War in Russia and Germany, 1812-13. Plans. 8vo. 14*s.*

CAVALCASELLE AND CROWE'S History of Painting in Italy, from the 2nd to the 16th Century. With Illustrations. 5 Vols. 8vo. 21*s.* each.

———— Early Flemish Painters, their Lives and Works. Illustrations. Post 8vo. 10*s.* 6*d.*; or Large Paper, 8vo. 15*s.*

CHILD (G. CHAPLIN, M.D.) Benedicite; or, the Song of the Three Children; being Illustrations of the Power, Beneficence, and Design manifested by the Creator in his works. *10th Thousand.* Post 8vo. 6*s.*

CHURTON'S (ARCHDEACON) Gongora. An Historical Essay on the Age of Philip III. and IV. of Spain. With Translations. Portrait. 2 Vols. Small 8vo. 12*s.*

———— New Testament. Edited with a Plain Practical Commentary for the use of Families and General Readers. With 100 Panoramic and other Views, from Sketches and Photographs made on the Spot. 2 vols. 8vo. 21*s.*

CICERO'S LIFE AND TIMES. His Character as a Statesman, Orator, and Friend, with a Selection from his Correspondence and Orations. By WILLIAM FORSYTH, LL.D. *Third Edition.* With Illustrations. 8vo. 10*s.* 6*d.*

CLARK'S (SIR JAMES) Memoir of Dr. John Conolly. Comprising a Sketch of the Treatment of the Insane in Europe and America. With Portrait. Post 8vo. 10*s.* 6*d.*

CHURCH (THE) & THE AGE. Essays on the Principles and Present Position of the Anglican Church. 8vo. 14s. Contents:—

Anglican Principles.—Dean Hook.
Modern Religious Thought.—Bishop of Gloucester and Bristol.
State, Church, and Synods.—Rev. Dr. Irons.
Religious Use of Taste.—Rev. R. St. John Tyrwhitt.
Place of the Laity.—Professor Burrows.
Parish Priest.—Rev. Walsham How.
Divines of 16th and 17th Centuries.—Rev. A. W. Haddan.
Liturgies and Ritual, Rev. M. F. Sadler.
Church & Education.—Canon Barry.
Indian Missions.—Sir Bartle Frere.
Church and the People.—Rev. W. D. Maclagan.
Conciliation and Comprehension.—Rev. Dr. Weir.

——— SECOND SERIES. 8vo. 12s. Contents:—

Church and Pauperism.—Earl Nelson.
American Church.—Bishop of Western New York.
Church and Science.—Prebendary Clark.
Ecclesiastical Law.—Isambard Brunel.
Church & National Education.—Canon Norris.
Church and Universities.—John G. Talbot.
Toleration.—Dean Cowie.
Eastern Church and Anglican Communion.—Rev. Geo. Williams.
A Disestablished Church.—Dean of Cashel.
Christian Tradition.—Rev. Dr. Irons.
Dogma.—Rev. Dr. Weir.
Parochial Councils.—Archdeacon Chapman.

CLIVE'S (LORD) Life. By REV. G. R. GLEIG. Post 8vo. 3s. 6d.

CLODE'S (C. M.) Military Forces of the Crown; their Administration and Government. 2 Vols. 8vo. 21s. each.

——— Administration of Justice under Military and Martial Law. 8vo. 12s.

COLCHESTER (THE) PAPERS. The Diary and Correspondence of Charles Abbott, Lord Colchester, Speaker of the House of Commons, 1802-1817. Portrait. 3 Vols. 8vo. 42s.

COLERIDGE'S (SAMUEL TAYLOR) Table-Talk. *Sixth Edition.* Portrait. Fcap. 8vo. 3s. 6d.

COLLINGWOOD'S (CUTHBERT) Rambles of a Naturalist on the Shores and Waters of the China Sea. Being Observations in Natural History during a Voyage to China, &c. With Illustrations. 8vo. 16s.

COLONIAL LIBRARY. [See Home and Colonial Library.]

COOK'S (Canon) Sermons Preached at Lincoln's Inn Chapel, and on Special Occasions. 8vo. 9s.

COOKERY (MODERN DOMESTIC). Founded on Principles of Economy and Practical Knowledge, and adapted for Private Families. By a Lady. *New Edition.* Woodcuts. Fcap. 8vo. 5s.

COOPER'S (T. T.) Travels of a Pioneer of Commerce on an Overland Journey from China towards India. Illustrations. 8vo. 16s.

CORNWALLIS (THE) Papers and Correspondence during the American War,—Administrations in India,—Union with Ireland, and Peace of Amiens. *Second Edition.* 3 Vols. 8vo. 63s.

COWPER'S (COUNTESS) Diary while Lady of the Bedchamber to Caroline Princess of Wales, 1714–20. Edited by Hon. SPENCER COWPER. *Second Edition.* Portrait. 8vo. 10s. 6d.

CRABBE'S (REV. GEORGE) Life and Poetical Works. With Illustrations. Royal 8vo. 7s.

CROKER'S (J. W.) Progressive Geography for Children. *Fifth Edition.* 18mo. 1*s.* 6*d.*

——— Stories for Children, Selected from the History of England. *Fifteenth Edition.* Woodcuts. 16mo. 2*s.* 6*d.*

——— Boswell's Life of Johnson. Including the Tour to the Hebrides. Portraits. Royal 8vo. 10*s.*

——— Essays on the Early Period of the French Revolution. 8vo. 15*s.*

——— Historical Essay on the Guillotine. Fcap. 8vo. 1*s.*

CROMWELL (OLIVER) and JOHN BUNYAN. Essays. By ROBERT SOUTHEY. Post 8vo. 2*s.*

CUMMING'S (R. GORDON) Five Years of a Hunter's Life in the Far Interior of South Africa; with Anecdotes of the Chace, and Notices of the Native Tribes. *Sixth Edition.* Woodcuts. Post 8vo. 6*s.*

CROWE'S AND CAVALCASELLE'S Lives of the Early Flemish Painters. Woodcuts. Post 8vo, 10*s.* 6*d.*; or Large Paper, 8vo, 15*s.*

——— History of Painting in Italy, from 2nd to 16th Century. Derived from Historical Researches as well as Inspection of the Works of Art in that Country. With more than 100 Illustrations. 5 Vols. 8vo. 21*s.* each.

CUNYNGHAME'S (SIR ARTHUR) Travels in the Eastern Caucasus, on the Caspian, and Black Seas, in Daghestan and the Frontiers of Persia and Turkey. With Map and Illustrations. 8vo. 18*s.*

CURTIUS' (PROFESSOR) Student's Greek Grammar, for the Upper Forms. Edited by DR. WM. SMITH. *Third Edition.* Post 8vo. 6*s.*

——— Elucidations of the above Grammar. Translated by EVELYN ABBOT. Post 8vo. 7*s.* 6*d.*

——— Smaller Greek Grammar for the Middle and Lower Forms. Abridged from the above. 12mo. 3*s.* 6*d.*

——— Accidence of the Greek Language. Extracted from the above work. 12mo. 2*s.* 6*d.*

——— Principles of Greek Etymology. Translated by A. S. WILKINS, M.A., and E. B. ENGLAND, B.A. Post 8vo.

CURZON'S (HON. ROBERT) ARMENIA AND ERZEROUM. A Year on the Frontiers of Russia, Turkey, and Persia. *Third Edition.* Woodcuts. Post 8vo. 7*s.* 6*d.*

——— Visits to the Monasteries of the Levant. *Fifth Edition.* Illustrations. Post 8vo. 7*s.* 6*d.*

CUST'S (GENERAL) Lives of the Warriors of the 17th Century—The Thirty Years' War. 2 Vols. 16*s.* Civil Wars of France and England. 2 Vols. 16*s.* Commanders of Fleets and Armies before the Enemy. 2 Vols. 18*s.*

——— Annals of the Wars—18th & 19th Century, 1700—1815. Compiled from the most Authentic Sources. With Maps. 9 Vols. Post 8vo. 5*s.* each.

DAVIS'S (NATHAN) Visit to the Ruined Cities of Numidia and Carthaginia. Illustrations. 8vo. 16*s.*

DAVY'S (SIR HUMPHRY) Consolations in Travel; or, Last Days of a Philosopher. *Seventh Edition.* Woodcuts. Fcap. 8vo. 3*s.* 6*d.*

——— Salmonia; or, Days of Fly Fishing. *Fifth Edition.* Woodcuts. Fcap. 8vo. 3*s.* 6*d.*

DE BEAUVOIR'S (MARQUIS) Voyage Round the World: touching at Australia, Java, Siam, Canton, Pekin, Jeddo, and San Francisco. 3 vols. Post 8vo.

DARWIN'S (CHARLES) Journal of Researches into the Natural History of the Countries visited during the Voyage of H.M.S. "Beagle" round the World. *Eleventh Thousand*. Post 8vo. 9*s*.

——— Origin of Species by Means of Natural Selection; or, the Preservation of Favoured Races in the Struggle for Life. *Sixth Edition*. Post 8vo. 7*s*. 6*d*.

——— Variation of Animals and Plants under Domestication. With Illustrations. 2 Vols. 8vo. 28*s*.

——— Descent of Man, and on Selection in Relation to Sex. With Illustrations. 2 Vols. Crown 8vo. 24*s*.

——— Expressions of the Emotions in Man and Animals. With Illustrations. Crown 8vo. 12*s*.

——— Fertilization of Orchids through Insect Agency, and as to the good of Intercrossing. Woodcuts. Post 8vo. 9*s*.

——— Fact and Argument for Darwin. By FRITZ MULLER. With numerous Illustrations and Additions by the Author. Translated from the German by W. S. DALLAS. Woodcuts. Post 8vo. 6*s*.

DELEPIERRE'S (OCTAVE) History of Flemish Literature. 8vo. 9*s*.

——— Historical Difficulties and Contested Events. Being Notes on some Doubtful Points of History. Post 8vo. 6*s*.

DENISON'S (E. B.) Life of Bishop Lonsdale. With Selections from his Writings. With Portrait. Crown 8vo. 10*s*. 6*d*.

DERBY'S (EARL OF) Iliad of Homer rendered into English Blank Verse. *7th Edition*. 2 Vols. Post 8vo. 10*s*.

DE ROS'S (LORD) Memorials of the Tower of London. *Second Edition*. With Illustrations. Crown 8vo. 12*s*.

——— Young Officer's Companion; or, Essays on Military Duties and Qualities: with Examples and Illustrations from History. Post 8vo. 9*s*.

DOG-BREAKING; the Most Expeditious, Certain, and Easy Method, whether great excellence or only mediocrity be required. With a Few Hints for those who Love the Dog and the Gun. By LIEUT.-GEN. HUTCHINSON. *Fifth Edition*. With 40 Woodcuts. Crown 8vo. 9*s*.

DOMESTIC MODERN COOKERY. Founded on Principles of Economy and Practical Knowledge, and adapted for Private Families. *New Edition*. Woodcuts. Fcap. 8vo. 5*s*.

DOUGLAS'S (SIR HOWARD) Life and Adventures. Portrait. 8vo. 15*s*.

——— Theory and Practice of Gunnery. *Fifth Edition*. Plates. 8vo. 21*s*.

——— Constructions of Bridges and the Passage of Rivers, in Military Operations. *Third Edition*. Plates. 8vo. 21*s*.

DRAKE'S (SIR FRANCIS) Life, Voyages, and Exploits, by Sea and Land. By JOHN BARROW. *Third Edition*. Post 8vo. 2*s*.

DRINKWATER'S (JOHN) History of the Siege of Gibraltar, 1779-1783. With a Description and Account of that Garrison from the Earliest Periods. Post 8vo. 2*s*.

DUCANGE'S MEDIÆVAL LATIN-ENGLISH DICTIONARY. Translated by Rev. E. A. DAYMAN, M.A. Small 4to. *(In preparation.)*

DU CHAILLU'S (PAUL B.) EQUATORIAL AFRICA, with Accounts of the Gorilla, the Nest-building Ape, Chimpanzee, Crocodile, &c. Illustrations. 8vo. 21*s*.

——— Journey to Ashango Land; and Further Penetration into Equatorial Africa. Illustrations. 8vo. 21*s*.

DUFFERIN'S (LORD) Letters from High Latitudes; an Account of a Yacht Voyage to Iceland, Jan Mayen, and Spitzbergen. *Fifth Edition.* Woodcuts. Post 8vo. 7*s*. 6*d*.

DUNCAN'S (CAPTAIN) History of the Royal Artillery. Compiled from the Original Records. Vol. 1 to the Peace of 1783. With Portrait. 8vo. 15*s*.

DYER'S (THOS. H.) History of Modern Europe, from the taking of Constantinople by the Turks to the close of the War in the Crimea. With Index. 4 Vols. 8vo. 42*s*.

EASTLAKE'S (SIR CHARLES) Italian Schools of Painting. From the German of KUGLER. Edited, with Notes. *Third Edition.* Illustrated from the Old Masters. 2 Vols. Post 8vo. 30*s*.

——— Contributions to the Literature of the Fine Arts. With Memoir of the Author, and Selections from his Correspondence. By LADY EASTLAKE. 2 Vols. 8vo. 24*s*.

EDWARDS' (W. H.) Voyage up the River Amazon, including a Visit to Para. Post 8vo. 2*s*.

ELDON'S (LORD) Public and Private Life, with Selections from his Correspondence and Diaries. By HORACE TWISS. *Third Edition.* Portrait. 2 Vols. Post 8vo. 21*s*.

ELGIN'S (LORD) Letters and Journals. Edited by THEODORE WALROND. *Second Edition.* 8vo. 14*s*.

ELLESMERE'S (LORD) Two Sieges of Vienna by the Turks. Translated from the German. Post 8vo. 2*s*.

ELLIS'S (W.) Madagascar, including a Journey to the Capital, with notices of Natural History and the People. Woodcuts. 8vo. 16*s*.

——— Revisited. Setting forth the Persecutions and Heroic Sufferings of the Native Christians. Illustrations. 8vo. 16*s*.

ELPHINSTONE'S (HON. MOUNTSTUART) History of India—the Hindoo and Mahomedan Periods. *Fifth Edition.* Map. 8vo. 18*s*.

——— (H. W.) Patterns for Turning; Comprising Elliptical and other Figures cut on the Lathe without the use of any Ornamental Chuck. With 70 Illustrations. Small 4to. 15*s*.

ENGEL'S (CARL) Music of the Most Ancient Nations; particularly of the Assyrians, Egyptians, and Hebrews; with Special Reference to the Discoveries in Western Asia and in Egypt. *Second Edition.* With 100 Illustrations. 8vo. 10*s*. 6*d*.

ENGLAND (HISTORY OF) See CALLCOTT, CROKER, HUME, MARKHAM, SMITH, and STANHOPE.

ENGLISHWOMAN IN AMERICA. Post 8vo. 10*s*. 6*d*.

ESSAYS ON CATHEDRALS. With an Introduction. By DEAN HOWSON. 8vo. 12*s*.

CONTENTS.

Recollections of a Dean.—Bishop of Carlisle.
Cathedral Canons and their Work.—Canon Norris.
Cathedrals in Ireland, Past and Future.—Dean of Cashel.
Cathedrals in their Missionary Aspect. A. J. B. Beresford Hope.
Cathedral Foundations in Relation to Religious Thought.—Canon Westcott.
Cathedral Churches of the Old Foundation.—Edward A. Freeman.
Welsh Cathedrals.—Canon Perowne.
Education of Choristers.—Sir F. Gore Ouseley.
Cathedral Schools.—Canon Durham.
Cathedral Reform.—Chancellor Massingberd.
Relation of the Chapter to the Bishop. Chancellor Benson.
Architecture of the Cathedral Churches.—Canon Venables.

ETHNOLOGICAL SOCIETY'S TRANSACTIONS. Vols. I. to VI. 8vo.

ELZE'S (KARL) Life of Lord Byron. With a Critical Essay on his Place in Literature. Translated from the German, and Edited with Notes. With Original Portrait and Facsimile. 8vo. 16*s*.

FAMILY RECEIPT-BOOK. A Collection of a Thousand Valuable and Useful Receipts. Fcap. 8vo. 5*s*. 6*d*.

FARRAR'S (A. S.) Critical History of Free Thought in reference to the Christian Religion. 8vo. 16*s*.

——— (F. W.) Origin of Language, based on Modern Researches. Fcap. 8vo. 5*s*.

FERGUSSON'S (JAMES) History of Architecture in all Countries from the Earliest Times. Vols. I. and II. With 1200 Illustrations. 8vo. 42*s*. each.

——— Rude Stone Monuments in all Countries; their Age and Uses. With 230 Illustrations. Medium 8vo. 24*s*.

——— Holy Sepulchre and the Temple at Jerusalem; being the Substance of Two Lectures delivered at the Royal Institution, 1862 and '65. Woodcuts. 8vo. 7*s*. 6*d*.

FLEMING'S (PROF.) Manual of Moral Philosophy. Post 8vo. 7*s*. 6*d*.

FLOWER GARDEN (THE). By REV. THOS. JAMES. Fcap. 8vo. 1*s*.

FONNEREAU'S (T. G.) Diary of a Dutiful Son. Fcap. 8vo. 4*s*. 6*d*.

FORSTER'S (JOHN) Arrest of the Five Members by Charles the First. A Chapter of English History re-written. Post 8vo.

——— Grand Remonstrance, 1641. With an Essay on English freedom under the Plantagenet and Tudor Sovereigns. *Second Edition*. Post 8vo. 12*s*.

——— Oliver Cromwell, Daniel De Foe, Sir Richard Steele, Charles Churchill, Samuel Foote. *Third Edition*. Post 8vo. 12*s*.

FORD'S (RICHARD) Gatherings from Spain. Post 8vo. 3*s*. 6*d*.

FORSYTH'S (WILLIAM) Life and Times of Cicero. With Selections from his Correspondence and Orations. *Third Edition*. Illustrations. 8vo. 10*s*. 6*d*.

——— History of Ancient Manuscripts. Post 8vo. 2*s*. 6*d*.

FORTUNE'S (ROBERT) Narrative of Two Visits to the Tea Countries of China, 1843-52. *Third Edition*. Woodcuts. 2 Vols. Post 8vo. 18*s*.

FOSS' (Edward) Judges of England. With Sketches of their Lives, and Notices of the Courts at Westminster, from the Conquest to the Present Time. 9 Vols. 8vo. 126*s*.

——— Biographia Juridica, or Biographical Dictionary of the Judges of England, from the Conquest to the Present Time, 1066-1870. (800 pp.) Medium 8vo. 21*s*.

——— Tabulæ Curiales; or, Tables of the Superior Courts of Westminster Hall. Showing the Judges who sat in them from 1066 to 1864. 8vo. 10*s*. 6*d*.

FRANCE (HISTORY OF). See MARKHAM, SMITH, Students.

FRENCH (THE) in Algiers; The Soldier of the Foreign Legion—and the Prisoners of Abd-el-Kadir. Translated by Lady DUFF GORDON. Post 8vo. 2*s*.

FRERE'S (SIR BARTLE) Results of Indian Missions. Small 8vo. 2*s.* 6*d.*

——— (M.) Old Deccan Days; or Fairy Legends Current in Southern India. Collected from Oral Tradition. With Notes, by SIR BARTLE FRERE. *Second Edition.* With Illustrations. Fcap. 8vo. 6*s.*

GALTON'S (FRANCIS) Art of Travel; or, Hints on the Shifts and Contrivances available in Wild Countries. *Fifth Edition.* Woodcuts. Post 8vo. 7*s.* 6*d.*

GEOGRAPHY. *** See Student's Manual.

GEOGRAPHICAL SOCIETY (JOURNAL OF). 8vo. 20*s.* (*Yearly.*)

GERMANY (HISTORY OF). See MARKHAM.

GIBBON'S (EDWARD) History of the Decline and Fall of the Roman Empire. Edited by MILMAN and GUIZOT. *A New Edition.* Preceded by his Autobiography. And Edited, with Notes, by Dr. WM. SMITH. Maps. 8 Vols. 8vo. 60*s.*

——— (The Student's Gibbon); Being an Epitome of the above work, incorporating the Researches of Recent Commentators. By Dr. WM. SMITH. Woodcuts. Post 8vo. 7*s.* 6*d.*

GIFFARD'S (EDWARD) Deeds of Naval Daring; or, Anecdotes of the British Navy. Fcap. 8vo. 3*s.* 6*d.*

GLADSTONE'S (W. E.) Financial Statements of 1853, 60, 63–65, and with Speeches on Tax-Bills and Charities. 8vo. 12*s.*

GLEIG'S (G. R.) Campaigns of the British Army at Washington and New Orleans. Post 8vo. 2*s.*

——— Story of the Battle of Waterloo. Post 8vo. 3*s.* 6*d.*

——— Narrative of Sale's Brigade in Affghanistan. Post 8vo. 2*s.*

——— Life of Robert Lord Clive. Post 8vo. 3*s.* 6*d.*

——— Sir Thomas Munro. Post 8vo. 3*s.* 6*d.*

GOLDSMITH'S (OLIVER) Works. A New Edition. Edited with Notes by PETER CUNNINGHAM. Vignettes. 4 Vols. 8vo. 30*s.*

GORDON'S (SIR ALEX.) Sketches of German Life, and Scenes from the War of Liberation. Post 8vo. 3*s.* 6*d.*

——— (LADY DUFF) Amber-Witch: A Trial for Witchcraft. Post 8vo. 2*s.*

——— French in Algiers. 1. The Soldier of the Foreign Legion. 2. The Prisoners of Abd-el-Kadir. Post 8vo. 2*s.*

GRAMMARS (ENGLISH, LATIN, and GREEK). See CURTIUS; HUTTON; MATTHIÆ; SMITH; KING EDWARD, &c.

GREECE (HISTORY OF). *See* GROTE—SMITH—Student.

GREY'S (EARL) Correspondence with King William IVth and Sir Herbert Taylor, from 1830 to 1832. 2 Vols. 8vo. 30*s.*

——— Parliamentary Government and Reform; with Suggestions for the Improvement of our Representative System. *Second Edition.* 8vo. 9*s.*

GRUNER'S (LEWIS) Terra-Cotta Architecture of North Italy, from careful Drawings and Restorations. With Illustrations, engraved and printed in Colours. Small folio. 5*l.* 5*s.*

GUIZOT'S (M.) Meditations on Christianity, and on the Religious Questions of the Day. Part I. The Essence. Part II. Present State. Part III. Relation to Society and Opinion. 3 Vols. Post 8vo. 30*s.*

GROTE'S (GEORGE) History of Greece. From the Earliest Times to the close of the generation contemporary with the death of Alexander the Great. *Fourth Edition.* Portrait, Maps, and Plans. 10 Vols. 8vo. 120*s.* Or, *Popular Edition.* Portrait and Plans. 12 Vols. Post 8vo. 6*s.* each.

——— PLATO, and the other Companions of Socrates. *Second Edition.* 3 Vols. 8vo. 45*s.*

——— Aristotle. Edited by ALEXANDER BAIN and G. CROOM ROBERTSON. 2 Vols. 8vo. 32*s.*

——— (MRS.) Personal Life of George Grote. Illustrated by numerous Letters. Portrait. 8vo.

——— Memoir of Ary Scheffer. *Second Edition.* With Portrait. 8vo. 8*s.* 6*d.*

HALLAM'S (HENRY) Constitutional History of England, from the Accession of Henry the Seventh to the Death of George the Second. *Seventh Edition.* 3 Vols. 8vo. 30*s.*, or 3 Vols. Post 8vo. 12*s.*

——— Student's Constitutional History of England. Edited by WM. SMITH, D.C.L. Post 8vo. 7*s.* 6*d.*

——— History of Europe during the Middle Ages. *Tenth Edition.* 3 Vols. 8vo. 30*s.*, or 3 Vols. Post 8vo. 12*s.*

——— Student's History of the Middle Ages. With Author's Supplemental Notes. Edited by WM. SMITH, D.C.L. Post 8vo. 7*s.* 6*d.*

——— Literary History of Europe, during the 15th, 16th and 17th Centuries. *Fourth Edition.* 3 Vols. 8vo. 36*s.*, or 4 Vols. Post 8vo. 16*s.*

——— (ARTHUR) Remains; in Verse and Prose. Portrait. Fcap. 8vo. 3*s.* 6*d.*

HANNAH'S (REV. DR.) Divine and Human Elements in Holy Scripture. 8vo. 10*s.* 6*d.*

HART'S ARMY LIST. (*Quarterly and Annually.*) 8vo.

HAY'S (SIR J. H. DRUMMOND) Western Barbary, its Wild Tribes and Savage Animals. Post 8vo. 2*s.*

HEAD'S (SIR FRANCIS) Royal Engineer. Illustrations. 8vo. 12*s.*

——— Life of Sir John Burgoyne. Post 8vo. 1*s.*

——— Rapid Journeys across the Pampas. Post 8vo. 2*s.*

——— Bubbles from the Brunnen of Nassau. *Seventh Edition.* Illustrations. Post 8vo. 7*s.* 6*d.*

——— Emigrant. Fcap. 8vo. 2*s.* 6*d.*

——— Stokers and Pokers; or, the London and North Western Railway. Post 8vo. 2*s.*

——— (SIR EDMUND) Shall and Will; or, Future Auxiliary Verbs. Fcap. 8vo. 4*s.*

HEBER'S (BISHOP) Journey through India from Calcutta to Bombay, Madras, &c. 2 Vols. Post 8vo. 7*s.*

——— Poetical Works. Portrait. Fcap. 8vo. 3*s.* 6*d.*

——— Hymns adapted to the Church Service. 16mo. 1*s.* 6*d.*

HERODOTUS. A New English Version. Edited, with Notes and Essays, historical, ethnographical, and geographical, by Rev. G. RAWLINSON, assisted by SIR HENRY RAWLINSON and SIR J. G. WILKINSON. *Second Edition.* Maps and Woodcuts. 4 Vols. 8vo. 48*s.*

FOREIGN HANDBOOKS.

HAND-BOOK—TRAVEL-TALK. English, French, German, and Italian. 18mo. 3*s*. 6*d*.

——— NORTH GERMANY,—HOLLAND, BELGIUM, PRUSSIA, and the Rhine from Holland to Switzerland. Map. Post 8vo. 12s.

——— SOUTH GERMANY, Bavaria, Austria, Styria, Salzburg, the Austrian and Bavarian Alps, the Tyrol, Hungary, and the Danube, from Ulm to the Black Sea. Map. Post 8vo. 12*s*.

——— KNAPSACK GUIDE TO THE TYROL. 16mo. 6*s*.

——— PAINTING. German, Flemish, and Dutch Schools. Illustrations. 2 Vols. Post 8vo. 24*s*.

——— LIVES OF EARLY FLEMISH PAINTERS. By CROWE and CAVALCASELLE. Illustrations. Post 8vo. 10*s*. 6d.

——— SWITZERLAND, Alps of Savoy, and Piedmont. Maps. Post 8vo. 10*s*. (*on thin paper*).

——— KNAPSACK GUIDE TO SWITZERLAND. 16mo, 5*s*.

——— FRANCE, Normandy, Brittany, the French Alps, the Rivers Loire, Seine, Rhone, and Garonne, Dauphiné, Provence, and the Pyrenees. Maps. Post 8vo.

——— CORSICA and SARDINIA. Maps. Post 8vo. 4*s*.

——— PARIS, and its Environs. Map and Plans. 16mo. 3*s*. 6*d*.

*** MURRAY'S PLAN OF PARIS, mounted on canvas. 3*s*. 6*d*.

——— SPAIN, Madrid, The Castiles, The Basque Provinces, Leon, The Asturias, Galicia, Estremadura, Andalusia, Ronda, Granada, Murcia, Valencia, Catalonia, Arragon, Navarre, The Balearic Islands, &c. &c. Maps. 2 Vols. Post 8vo. 24*s*.

——— PORTUGAL, LISBON, Porto, Cintra, Mafra, &c. Map. Post 8vo. 9*s*.

——— NORTH ITALY, Piedmont, Liguria, Venetia, Lombardy, Parma, Modena, and Romagna. Map. Post 8vo. 12*s*. (*on thin paper*).

——— CENTRAL ITALY, Lucca, Tuscany, Florence, The Marches, Umbria, and the Patrimony of St. Peter's. Map. Post 8vo. 10*s*.

——— ROME AND ITS ENVIRONS. Map. Post 8vo. 10*s*.

——— SOUTH ITALY, Two Sicilies, Naples, Pompeii, Herculaneum, and Vesuvius. Map. Post 8vo. 10*s*.

——— KNAPSACK GUIDE TO ITALY. 16mo. 6*s*.

——— SICILY, Palermo, Messina, Catania, Syracuse, Etna, and the Ruins of the Greek Temples. Map. Post 8vo. 12*s*.

——— PAINTING. The Italian Schools. Edited by Sir CHARLES EASTLAKE, R.A. Illustrations. 2 Vols. Post 8vo. 30*s*.

——— LIVES OF ITALIAN PAINTERS, FROM CIMABUE to BASSANO. By Mrs. JAMESON. Portraits. Post 8vo. 12*s*.

——— RUSSIA, ST. PETERSBURGH, MOSCOW, POLAND, and FINLAND. Maps. Post 8vo. 15*s*.

HAND-BOOK—DENMARK, SWEDEN, and NORWAY. Maps. Post 8vo. 15s.

——— KNAPSACK GUIDE TO NORWAY. Map. 12mo. 6s.

——— GREECE, the Ionian Islands, Continental Greece, Athens, the Peloponnesus, the Islands of the Ægean Sea, Albania, Thessaly, and Macedonia. Maps. Post 8vo. 15s.

——— TURKEY IN ASIA—CONSTANTINOPLE, the Bosphorus, Dardanelles, Brousa, Plain of Troy, Crete, Cyprus, Smyrna, Ephesus, the Seven Churches, Coasts of the Black Sea, Armenia, Mesopotamia, &c. Maps. Post 8vo. 15s.

——— EGYPT, including Descriptions of the Course of the Nile through Egypt and Nubia, Alexandria, Cairo, and Thebes, the Suez Canal, the Pyramids, the Peninsula of Sinai, the Oases, the Fyoom, &c. Map. Post 8vo. 15s.

——— HOLY LAND—SYRIA AND PALESTINE, Peninsula of Sinai, Edom, and Syrian Desert. Maps. 2 Vols. Post 8vo. 24s.

——— INDIA — BOMBAY AND MADRAS. Map. 2 Vols. Post 8vo. 12s. each.

ENGLISH HANDBOOKS.

HAND-BOOK—MODERN LONDON. Map. 16mo. 3s. 6d.

——— ESSEX, CAMBRIDGE, SUFFOLK, AND NORFOLK, Chelmsford, Colchester, Maldon, Cambridge, Ely, Newmarket, Bury, Ipswich, Woodbridge, Felixstowe, Lowestoft, Norwich, Yarmouth, Cromer, &c. Map and Plans. Post 8vo. 12s.

——— CATHEDRALS of Oxford, Peterborough, Norwich, Ely, and Lincoln. With 90 Illustrations. Crown 8vo. 18s.

——— KENT AND SUSSEX, Canterbury, Dover, Ramsgate, Sheerness, Rochester, Chatham, Woolwich, Brighton, Chichester, Worthing, Hastings, Lewes, Arundel, &c. Map. Post 8vo. 10s.

——— SURREY AND HANTS, Kingston, Croydon, Reigate, Guildford, Dorking, Boxhill, Winchester, Southampton, New Forest, Portsmouth, and ISLE OF WIGHT. Maps. Post 8vo. 10s.

——— BERKS, BUCKS, AND OXON, Windsor, Eton, Reading, Aylesbury, Uxbridge, Wycombe, Henley, the City and University of Oxford, Blenheim, and the Descent of the Thames. Map. Post 8vo. 7s. 6d.

——— WILTS, DORSET, AND SOMERSET, Salisbury, Chippenham, Weymouth, Sherborne, Wells, Bath, Bristol, Taunton, &c. Map. Post 8vo. 10s.

——— DEVON AND CORNWALL, Exeter, Ilfracombe, Linton, Sidmouth, Dawlish, Teignmouth, Plymouth, Devonport, Torquay, Launceston, Truro, Penzance, Falmouth, the Lizard, Land's End, &c. Maps. Post 8vo. 12s.

——— CATHEDRALS of Winchester, Salisbury, Exeter, Wells, Chichester, Rochester, Canterbury. With 110 Illustrations. 2 Vols. Crown 8vo. 24s.

——— GLOUCESTER, HEREFORD, AND WORCESTER, Cirencester, Cheltenham, Stroud, Tewkesbury, Leominster, Ross, Malvern, Kidderminster, Dudley, Bromsgrove, Evesham. Map. Post 8vo. 9s.

——— CATHEDRALS of Bristol, Gloucester, Hereford, Worcester, and Lichfield. With 50 Illustrations. Crown 8vo. 16s.

——— NORTH WALES, Bangor, Carnarvon, Beaumaris, Snowdon, Llanberis, Dolgelly, Cader Idris, Conway, &c. Map. Post 8vo. 6s. 6d.

HAND-BOOK—SOUTH WALES, Monmouth, Llandaff, Merthyr, Vale of Neath, Pembroke, Carmarthen, Tenby, Swansea, and The Wye, &c. Map. Post 8vo. 7*s.*

——— CATHEDRALS OF BANGOR, ST. ASAPH, Llandaff, and St. Davids. With Illustrations. Post 8vo. 15*s.*

——— DERBY, NOTTS, LEICESTER, STAFFORD, Matlock, Bakewell, Chatsworth, The Peak, Buxton, Hardwick, Dove Dale, Ashborne, Southwell, Mansfield, Retford, Burton, Belvoir, Melton Mowbray, Wolverhampton, Lichfield, Walsall, Tamworth. Map. Post 8vo. 7*s.* 6*d.*

——— SHROPSHIRE, CHESHIRE AND LANCASHIRE —Shrewsbury, Ludlow, Bridgnorth, Oswestry, Chester, Crewe, Alderley, Stockport, Birkenhead, Warrington, Bury, Manchester, Liverpool, Burnley, Clitheroe, Bolton, Blackburn, Wigan, Preston, Rochdale, Lancaster, Southport, Blackpool, &c. Map. Post 8vo. 10*s.*

——— YORKSHIRE, Doncaster, Hull, Selby, Beverley, Scarborough, Whitby, Harrogate, Ripon, Leeds, Wakefield, Bradford, Halifax, Huddersfield, Sheffield. Map and Plans. Post 8vo. 12*s.*

——— CATHEDRALS of York, Ripon, Durham, Carlisle, Chester, and Manchester. With 60 Illustrations. 2 Vols. Crown 8vo. 21*s.*

——— DURHAM AND NORTHUMBERLAND, Newcastle, Darlington, Gateshead, Bishop Auckland, Stockton, Hartlepool, Sunderland, Shields, Berwick-on-Tweed, Morpeth, Tynemouth, Coldstream, Alnwick, &c. Map. Post 8vo.

——— WESTMORLAND AND CUMBERLAND—Lancaster, Furness Abbey, Ambleside, Kendal, Windermere, Coniston, Keswick, Grasmere, Ulswater, Carlisle, Cockermouth, Penrith, Appleby. Map. Post 8vo. 6*s.*

*** MURRAY'S MAP OF THE LAKE DISTRICT, on canvas. 3*s.* 6*d.*

——— SCOTLAND, Edinburgh, Melrose, Kelso, Glasgow, Dumfries, Ayr, Stirling, Arran, The Clyde, Oban, Inverary, Loch Lomond, Loch Katrine and Trossachs, Caledonian Canal, Inverness, Perth, Dundee, Aberdeen, Braemar, Skye, Caithness, Ross, Sutherland, &c. Maps and Plans. Post 8vo.

——— IRELAND, Dublin, Belfast, Donegal, Galway, Wexford, Cork, Limerick, Waterford, Killarney, Munster, &c. Maps. Post 8vo. 12*s.*

HAND-BOOK OF FAMILIAR QUOTATIONS. From English Authors. *Third Edition.* Fcap. 8vo. 5*s.*

HATHERLEY (LORD) On the Continuity of Scripture. As declared by the Testimony of our Lord and of the Evangelists and Apostles. *Fourth Edition.* 8vo. 6*s.* Or *Popular Edition.* Post 8vo. 2*s.* 6*d.*

HESSEY (REV. DR.). Sunday—Its Origin, History, and Present Obligations. Post 8vo. 9*s.*

HICKMAN'S (WM.) Treatise on the Law and Practice of Naval Courts-Martial. 8vo. 10*s.* 6*d.*

HOLLWAY'S (J. G.) Month in Norway. Fcap. 8vo. 2*s.*

HONEY BEE (THE). An Essay. By REV. THOMAS JAMES. Reprinted from the "Quarterly Review." Fcap. 8vo. 1*s.*

HOOK'S (DEAN) Church Dictionary. *Tenth Edition.* 8vo. 16*s.*

——— (THEODORE) Life. By J. G. LOCKHART. Fcap. 8vo. 1*s.*

HOPE'S ARCHITECTURE OF AHMEDABAD, with Historical Sketch and Architectural Notes by T. C. HOPE, and JAMES FERGUSSON, F.R.S. With 2 Maps, 120 Photographs and 22 Woodcuts. 4to. 5*l.* 5*s.*

HOME AND COLONIAL LIBRARY. A Series of Works adapted for all circles and classes of Readers, having been selected for their acknowledged interest, and ability of the Authors. Post 8vo. Published at 2*s*. and 3*s*. 6*d*. each, and arranged under two distinctive heads as follows:—

CLASS A.

HISTORY, BIOGRAPHY, AND HISTORIC TALES.

1. SIEGE OF GIBRALTAR. By JOHN DRINKWATER. 2*s*.
2. THE AMBER-WITCH. By LADY DUFF GORDON. 2*s*.
3. CROMWELL AND BUNYAN. By ROBERT SOUTHEY. 2*s*.
4. LIFE OF SIR FRANCIS DRAKE. By JOHN BARROW. 2*s*.
5. CAMPAIGNS AT WASHINGTON. By REV. G. R. GLEIG. 2*s*.
6. THE FRENCH IN ALGIERS. By LADY DUFF GORDON. 2*s*.
7. THE FALL OF THE JESUITS. 2*s*.
8. LIVONIAN TALES. 2*s*.
9. LIFE OF CONDE. By LORD MAHON. 3*s*. 6*d*.
10. SALE'S BRIGADE. By REV. G. R. GLEIG. 2*s*.
11. THE SIEGES OF VIENNA. By LORD ELLESMERE. 2*s*.
12. THE WAYSIDE CROSS. By CAPT. MILMAN. 2*s*.
13. SKETCHES OF GERMAN LIFE. By SIR A. GORDON. 3*s*. 6*d*.
14. THE BATTLE OF WATERLOO. By REV. G. R. GLEIG. 3*s*. 6*d*.
15. AUTOBIOGRAPHY OF STEFFENS. 2*s*.
16. THE BRITISH POETS. By THOMAS CAMPBELL. 3*s*. 6*d*.
17. HISTORICAL ESSAYS. By LORD MAHON. 3*s*. 6*d*.
18. LIFE OF LORD CLIVE. By REV. G. R. GLEIG. 3*s*. 6*d*.
19. NORTH - WESTERN RAILWAY. By SIR F. B. HEAD. 2*s*.
20. LIFE OF MUNRO. By REV. G. R. GLEIG. 3*s*. 6*d*.

CLASS B.

VOYAGES, TRAVELS, AND ADVENTURES.

1. BIBLE IN SPAIN. By GEORGE BORROW. 3*s*. 6*d*.
2. GIPSIES OF SPAIN. By GEORGE BORROW. 3*s*. 6*d*.

3 & 4. JOURNALS IN INDIA. By BISHOP HEBER. 2 Vols. 7*s*.

5. TRAVELS IN THE HOLY LAND. By IRBY and MANGLES. 2*s*.
6. MOROCCO AND THE MOORS. By J. DRUMMOND HAY. 2*s*.
7. LETTERS FROM THE BALTIC. By A LADY. 2*s*.
8. NEW SOUTH WALES. By MRS. MEREDITH. 2*s*.
9. THE WEST INDIES. By M. G. LEWIS. 2*s*.
10. SKETCHES OF PERSIA. By SIR JOHN MALCOLM. 3*s*. 6*d*.
11. MEMOIRS OF FATHER RIPA. 2*s*.

12, 13. TYPEE AND OMOO. By HERMANN MELVILLE. 2 Vols. 7*s*.

14. MISSIONARY LIFE IN CANADA. By REV. J. ABBOTT. 2*s*.
15. LETTERS FROM MADRAS. By A LADY. 2*s*.
16. HIGHLAND SPORTS. By CHARLES ST. JOHN. 3*s*. 6*d*.
17. PAMPAS JOURNEYS. By SIR F. B. HEAD. 2*s*.
18. GATHERINGS FROM SPAIN. By RICHARD FORD. 3*s*. 6*d*.
19. THE RIVER AMAZON. By W. H. EDWARDS. 2*s*.
20. MANNERS & CUSTOMS OF INDIA. By REV. C. ACLAND. 2*s*.
21. ADVENTURES IN MEXICO. By G. F. RUXTON. 3*s*. 6*d*.
22. PORTUGAL AND GALLICIA. By LORD CARNARVON. 3*s*. 6*d*.
23. BUSH LIFE IN AUSTRALIA. By REV. H. W. HAYGARTH. 2*s*.
24. THE LIBYAN DESERT. By BAYLE ST. JOHN. 2*s*.
25. SIERRA LEONE. By LADY. 3*s*. 6*d*.

*** Each work may be had separately.

HORACE; a New Edition of the Text. Edited by DEAN MILMAN. With 100 Woodcuts. Crown 8vo. 7*s.* 6*d.*

——— Life of. By DEAN MILMAN. Illustrations. 8vo. 9*s.*

HOUGHTON'S (LORD) Monographs, Personal and Social. With Portraits. Crown 8vo.

HUME'S History of England, from the Invasion of Julius Cæsar to the Revolution of 1688. Corrected and continued to 1868. Abridged for Students. Edited by DR. WM. SMITH. Woodcuts. Post 8vo. 7*s.* 6*d.*

HUTCHINSON (GEN.), on the most expeditious, certain, and easy Method of Dog-Breaking. *Fifth Edition.* With 40 Illustrations. Crown 8vo. 9*s.*

HUTTON'S (H. E.) Principia Græca; an Introduction to the Study of Greek. Comprehending Grammar, Delectus, and Exercise-book, with Vocabularies. *Sixth Edition.* 12mo. 3*s.* 6*d.*

IRBY AND MANGLES' Travels in Egypt, Nubia, Syria, and the Holy Land. Post 8vo. 2*s.*

JAMES' (REV. THOMAS) Fables of Æsop. A New Translation, with Historical Preface. With 100 Woodcuts by TENNIEL and WOLF. *Sixty-fourth Thousand.* Post 8vo. 2*s.* 6*d.*

JAMESON'S (MRS.) Lives of the Early Italian Painters—and the Progress of Painting in Italy—Cimabue to Bassano. *New Edition.* With 50 Portraits. Post 8vo. 12*s.*

JENNINGS' (L. J.) Eighty Years of Republican Government in the United States. Post 8vo. 10*s.* 6*d.*

JESSE'S (EDWARD) Gleanings in Natural History. *Eleventh Edition.* Fcp. 8vo. 3*s.* 6*d.*

JOHNS' (REV. B. G.) Blind People; their Works and Ways. With Sketches of the Lives of some famous Blind Men. With Illustrations. Post 8vo. 7*s.* 6*d.*

JOHNSON'S (DR. SAMUEL) Life. By James Boswell. Including the Tour to the Hebrides. Edited by MR. CROKER. Portraits. Royal 8vo. 10*s.*

——— Lives of the most eminent English Poets. Edited with Notes by PETER CUNNINGHAM. 3 vols. 8vo. 22*s.* 6*d.*

JUNIUS' HANDWRITING Professionally investigated. By Mr. CHABOT, Expert. With Preface and Collateral Evidence, by the Hon. EDWARD TWISLETON. With Facsimiles, Woodcuts, &c. 4to. £3 3*s.*

KEN'S (BISHOP) Life. By a LAYMAN. Portrait. 2 Vols. 8vo. 18*s.*

——— Exposition of the Apostles' Creed. 16mo. 1*s.* 6*d.*

KERR'S (ROBERT) GENTLEMAN'S HOUSE; OR, HOW TO PLAN ENGLISH RESIDENCES, FROM THE PARSONAGE TO THE PALACE. *Third Edition.* With Views and Plans. 8vo. 24*s.*

——— Ancient Lights; a Book for Architects, Surveyors, Lawyers, and Landlords. 8vo. 5*s.* 6*d.*

——— (R. MALCOLM) Student's Blackstone. A Systematic Abridgment of the entire Commentaries, adapted to the present state of the law. Post 8vo. 7*s.* 6*d.*

KING EDWARD VITH'S Latin Grammar; or, an Introduction to the Latin Tongue. *Seventeenth Edition.* 12mo. 3*s.* 6*d.*

——— First Latin Book; or, the Accidence, Syntax, and Prosody, with an English Translation. *Fifth Edition.* 12mo. 2*s.* 6*d.*

KING GEORGE THE THIRD'S CORRESPONDENCE WITH LORD NORTH, 1769-82. Edited, with Notes and Introduction, by W. BODHAM DONNE. 2 vols. 8vo. 32*s*.

KIRK'S (J. FOSTER) History of Charles the Bold, Duke of Burgundy. Portrait. 3 Vols. 8vo. 45*s*.

KIRKES' Handbook of Physiology. Edited by W. MORRANT BAKER, F.R.C.S. *Eighth Edition.* With 240 Illustrations. Post 8vo. 12*s*. 6*d*.

KUGLER'S Italian Schools of Painting. Edited, with Notes, by SIR CHARLES EASTLAKE. *Third Edition.* Woodcuts. 2 Vols. Post 8vo. 30*s*.

——— German, Dutch, and Flemish Schools of Painting. Edited, with Notes, by DR. WAAGEN. *Second Edition.* Woodcuts. 2 Vols. Post 8vo. 24*s*.

LANE'S (E. W.) Account of the Manners and Customs of the Modern Egyptians. *New Edition.* With Illustrations. 2 Vols. Post 8vo. 12*s*.

LAYARD'S (A. H.) Nineveh and its Remains. Being a Narrative of Researches and Discoveries amidst the Ruins of Assyria. With an Account of the Chaldean Christians of Kurdistan; the Yezedis, or Devil-worshippers; and an Enquiry into the Manners and Arts of the Ancient Assyrians. *Sixth Edition.* Plates and Woodcuts. 2 Vols. 8vo. 36*s*.

*** A POPULAR EDITION of the above work. With Illustrations. Post 8vo. 7*s*. 6*d*.

——— Nineveh and Babylon; being the Narrative of Discoveries in the Ruins, with Travels in Armenia, Kurdistan and the Desert, during a Second Expedition to Assyria. With Map and Plates. 8vo. 21*s*.

*** A POPULAR EDITION of the above work. With Illustrations. Post 8vo. 7*s*. 6*d*.

LEATHES' (STANLEY) Practical Hebrew Grammar. With an Appendix, containing the Hebrew Text of Genesis i.—vi., and Psalms i.—vi. Grammatical Analysis and Vocabulary. Post 8vo. 7*s*. 6*d*.

LENNEP'S (REV. H. J. VAN) Missionary Travels in Asia Minor. With Illustrations of Biblical History and Archæology. With Map and Woodcuts. 2 Vols. Post 8vo. 24*s*.

LESLIE'S (C. R.) Handbook for Young Painters. *Second Edition.* With Illustrations. Post 8vo. 7*s*. 6*d*.

——— Life and Works of Sir Joshua Reynolds. Portraits and Illustrations. 2 Vols. 8vo. 42*s*.

LETTERS FROM THE BALTIC. By a LADY. Post 8vo. 2*s*.

——— MADRAS. By a LADY. Post 8vo. 2*s*.

——— SIERRA LEONE. By a LADY. Post 8vo. 3*s*. 6*d*.

LEVI'S (LEONE) Wages and Earnings of the Working Classes. With some Facts Illustrative of their Economic Condition. 8vo. 6*s*.

——— History of British Commerce; and of the Economic Progress of the Nation, from 1763 to 1870. 8vo. 16*s*.

LEWIS'S (M. G.) Journal of a Residence among the Negroes in the West Indies. Post 8vo. 2*s*.

LIDDELL'S (DEAN) Student's History of Rome, from the earliest Times to the establishment of the Empire. With Woodcuts. Post 8vo. 7*s*. 6*d*.

LINDSAY'S (LORD) Lives of the Lindsays; or, a Memoir of the Houses of Crawfurd and Balcarres. With Extracts from Official Papers and Personal Narratives. *Second Edition.* 3 Vols. 8vo. 24*s*.

——— Etruscan Inscriptions. Analysed, Translated, and Commented upon. 8vo. 12*s*.

LLOYD'S (W. WATKISS) History of Sicily to the Athenian War; with Elucidations of the Sicilian Odes of Pindar. With a Map. 8vo. 14*s.*

LISPINGS from LOW LATITUDES; or, the Journal of the Hon. Impulsia Gushington. Edited by LORD DUFFERIN. With 24 Plates. 4to. 21*s.*

LITTLE ARTHUR'S HISTORY OF ENGLAND. By LADY CALLCOTT. *New Edition, continued to* 1871. With Woodcuts. Fcap. 8vo. 2*s.* 6*d.*

LIVINGSTONE'S (DR.) Missionary Travels in South Africa. Illustrations. Post 8vo. 6*s.*

——— Expedition to the Zambezi and its Tributaries; and the Lakes Shirwa and Nyassa. Map and Illustrations. 8vo. 21*s.*

LIVONIAN TALES. By the Author of "Letters from the Baltic." Post 8vo. 2*s.*

LOCH'S (H. B.) Personal Narrative of Events during Lord Elgin's Second Embassy to China. *Second Edition.* With Illustrations. Post 8vo. 9*s.*

LOCKHART'S (J. G.) Ancient Spanish Ballads. Historical and Romantic. Translated, with Notes. *New Edition.* With Portrait and Illustrations. Crown 8vo. 5*s.*

——— Life of Theodore Hook. Fcap. 8vo. 1*s.*

LONSDALE'S (BISHOP) Life. With Selections from his Writings. By E. B. DENISON. With Portrait. Crown 8vo. 10*s.* 6*d.*

LOUDON'S (MRS.) Gardening for Ladies. With Directions and Calendar of Operations for Every Month. *Eighth Edition.* Woodcuts. Fcap. 8vo. 3*s.* 6*d.*

LUCKNOW: a Lady's Diary of the Siege. Fcap. 8vo. 4*s.* 6*d.*

LYELL'S (SIR CHARLES) Principles of Geology; or, the Modern Changes of the Earth and its Inhabitants considered as illustrative of Geology. *Tenth Edition.* With Illustrations. 2 Vols. 8vo. 32*s.*

——— Student's Elements of Geology. With 600 Illustrations. Post 8vo. 9*s.*

——— Geological Evidences of the Antiquity of Man. *Fourth Edition.* Illustrations. 8vo. (*In Preparation.*)

——— (K. M.) Geographical Handbook of Ferns. With Tables to show their Distribution. Post 8vo. 7*s.* 6*d.*

LYTTELTON'S (LORD) Ephemera. *1st & 2nd Series.* Post 8vo. 10*s.* 6*d.* each.

LYTTON'S (LORD) Poems. Post 8vo. 10*s.* 6*d.*

——— Lost Tales of Miletus. Post 8vo. 7*s.* 6*d.*

——— Memoir of Julian Fane. *Second Edition.* With Portrait. Post 8vo. 5*s.*

McCLINTOCK'S (SIR L.) Narrative of the Discovery of the Fate of Sir John Franklin and his Companions in the Arctic Seas. *Third Edition.* With Illustrations. Post 8vo. 7*s.* 6*d.*

MACDOUGALL'S (COL.) Modern Warfare as Influenced by Modern Artillery. With Plans. Post 8vo. 12*s.*

MACGREGOR (J.), Rob Roy on the Jordan, Nile, Red Sea, Gennesareth, &c. A Canoe Cruise in Palestine and Egypt and the Waters of Damascus. With Map, and 70 Illustrations. Crown 8vo. 12*s.*

MACPHERSON'S (MAJOR) Services in India, while Political Agent at Gwalior during the Mutiny. Illustrations. 8vo. 12*s.*

MAETZNER'S COPIOUS ENGLISH GRAMMAR. A Methodical, Analytical, and Historical Treatise on the Orthography, Prosody, Inflections, and Syntax of the English Tongue. 3 Vols. 8vo. (*In preparation.*)

MAHON (LORD), see STANHOPE.

MAINE'S (SIR H. SUMNER) Ancient Law: its Connection with the Early History of Society, and its Relation to Modern Ideas. *Fourth Edition.* 8vo. 12*s*.

——— VILLAGE COMMUNITIES IN THE EAST AND WEST. *2nd Edition.* 8vo. 9*s*.

MALCOLM'S (SIR JOHN) Sketches of Persia. Post 8vo. 3*s*. 6*d*.

MANSEL'S (DEAN) Limits of Religious Thought Examined. *Fifth Edition.* Post 8vo. 8*s*. 6*d*.

——— Letters, Lectures, and Papers. 8vo.

MANTELL'S (GIDEON A.) Thoughts on Animalcules; or, the Invisible World, as revealed by the Microscope. Plates. 16mo. 6*s*.

MANUAL OF SCIENTIFIC ENQUIRY. For the Use of Travellers. Edited by SIR J. F. HERSCHEL & REV. R. MAIN. Post 8vo. 3*s*. 6*d*. (*Published by order of the Lords of the Admiralty.*)

MARCO POLO'S TRAVELS. A New English Version. With Copious Illustrative Notes. By COL. HENRY YULE. With Maps and Illustrations. 2 Vols. Medium 8vo. 42*s*.

MARKHAM'S (MRS.) History of England. From the First Invasion by the Romans. *New Edition, continued down to* 1867. Woodcuts. 12mo. 3*s*. 6*d*.

——— History of France. From the Conquest by the Gauls. *New Edition, continued to* 1867. Woodcuts. 12mo. 3*s*. 6*d*.

——— History of Germany. From the Invasion by Marius. *New Edition, continued to* 1867. Woodcuts. 12mo.

——— (CLEMENTS R.) Travels in Peru and India. Maps and Illustrations. 8vo. 16*s*.

MARRYAT'S (JOSEPH) History of Modern and Mediæval Pottery and Porcelain. With a Description of the Manufacture. *Third Edition.* Plates and Woodcuts. 8vo. 42*s*.

MARSH'S (G. P.) Manual of the English Language. Edited by DR. WM. SMITH. Post 8vo. 7*s*. 6*d*.

MATTHIÆ'S SHORTER GREEK GRAMMAR. Abridged by BISHOP BLOMFIELD. *A New Edition, revised and enlarged* by E. S. CROOKE. 12mo. 4*s*.

MAUREL, on the Character, Actions, and Writings of Wellington. Fcap. 8vo. 1*s*. 6*d*.

MAYNE'S (CAPT.) Four Years in British Columbia and Vancouver Island. Illustrations. 8vo. 16*s*.

MEADE'S (HON. HERBERT) Ride through the Disturbed Districts of New Zealand to Lake Taupo, at the Time of the Rebellion; with a Cruise among the South Sea Islands. With Illustrations. Medium 8vo. 14*s*.

MELVILLE'S (HERMANN) Adventures amongst the Marquesas and South Sea Islands. 2 Vols. Post 8vo. 7*s*.

MEREDITH'S (MRS. CHARLES) Notes and Sketches of New South Wales. Post 8vo. 2*s*.

MESSIAH (THE): A Narrative of the Life, Travels, Death, Resurrection, and Ascension of our Blessed Lord. By A Layman. Map. 8vo. 18*s*.

MILLS' (REV. JOHN) Three Months' Residence at Nablus, with an Account of the Modern Samaritans. Illustrations. Post 8vo. 10*s*. 6*d*.

MILMAN'S (DEAN) History of the Jews, from the earliest Period down to Modern Times. 3 Vols. Post 8vo. 18*s*.

——— History of Early Christianity, from the Birth of Christ to the Abolition of Paganism in the Roman Empire. *Fourth Edition*. 3 Vols. Post 8vo. 18*s*.

——— History of Latin Christianity, including that of the Popes to the Pontificate of Nicholas V. *Fourth Edition*. 9 Vols. Post 8vo. 54*s*.

——— Annals of St. Paul's Cathedral, from the time of the Romans to the funeral of the Duke of Wellington. *Second Edition*. Portrait and Illustrations. 8vo. 18*s*.

——— Character and Conduct of the Apostles considered as an Evidence of Christianity. 8vo. 10*s*. 6*d*.

——— Quinti Horatii Flacci Opera. *New Edition*. With 100 Woodcuts. Small 8vo. 7*s*. 6*d*.

——— Life of Quintus Horatius Flaccus. *Second Edition*. With Illustrations. 8vo. 9*s*.

——— Poetical Works. The Fall of Jerusalem—Martyr of Antioch—Balshazzar—Tamor—Anne Boleyn—Fazio, &c. With Portraits and Illustrations. 3 Vols. Fcap. 8vo. 18*s*.

——— Fall of Jerusalem. Fcap. 8vo. 1*s*.

——— (CAPT. E. A.) Wayside Cross. Post 8vo. 2*s*.

MICHIE'S (ALEXANDER) Siberian Overland Route from Peking to Petersburg. Maps and Illustrations. 8vo. 16*s*.

MODERN DOMESTIC COOKERY. Founded on Principles of Economy and Practical Knowledge. *New Edition*. Woodcuts. Fcap. 8vo. 5*s*.

MONGREDIEN'S (AUGUSTUS) Trees and Shrubs for English Plantation. A Selection and Description of the most Ornamental which will flourish in the open air in our climate. With Classified Lists. With 30 Illustrations. 8vo. 16*s*.

MOORE & JACKMAN on the Clematis as a Garden Flower. Descriptions of the Hardy Species and Varieties, with Directions for their Cultivation, and purposes for which they are adapted in Modern Gardening. Plates. 8vo. 10*s*. 6*d*.

MOORE'S (THOMAS) Life and Letters of Lord Byron. *Cabinet Edition*. With Plates. 6 Vols. Fcap. 8vo. 18*s*.; or *Popular Edition*, with Portraits. Royal 8vo. 9*s*.

MOTLEY'S (J. L.) History of the United Netherlands: from the Death of William the Silent to the Twelve Years' Truce, 1609. *Library Edition*. Portraits. 4 Vols. 8vo. 60*s*. Or *Cabinet Edition*, 4 Vols. Post 8vo. 6*s*. each.

MOUHOT'S (HENRI) Siam, Cambojia, and Lao; a Narrative of Travels and Discoveries. Illustrations. 2 vols. 8vo.

MOZLEY'S (CANON) Treatise on Predestination. 8vo. 14*s*.

——— Primitive Doctrine of Baptismal Regeneration. 8vo. 7*s*.6*d*.

MUNDY'S (GENERAL) Pen and Pencil Sketches in India. *Third Edition*. Plates. Post 8vo. 7*s*. 6*d*.

MUNRO'S (GENERAL) Life and Letters. By REV. G. R. GLEIG. Post 8vo. 3*s*. 6*d*.

MURCHISON'S (SIR RODERICK) Russia in Europe and the Ural Mountains. With Coloured Maps, &c. 2 Vols. 4to. 5*l*. 5*s*.

——— Siluria; or, a History of the Oldest Rocks containing Organic Remains. *Fifth Edition*. Map and Plates. 8vo. 18*s*.

MURRAY'S RAILWAY READING. Containing:—

Wellington. By Lord Ellesmere. 6*d*.
Nimrod on the Chase, 1*s*.
Music and Dress. 1*s*.
Milman's Fall of Jerusalem. 1*s*.
Mahon's "Forty-Five." 3*s*.
Life of Theodore Hook. 1*s*.
Deeds of Naval Daring. 3*s*. 6*d*.
The Honey Bee. 1*s*.
James' Æsop's Fables. 2*s*. 6*d*.
Nimrod on the Turf. 1*s*. 6*d*.
Art of Dining. 1*s*. 6*d*.
Mahon's Joan of Arc. 1*s*.
Head's Emigrant. 2*s*. 6*d*.
Nimrod on the Road. 1*s*.
Croker on the Guillotine. 1*s*.
Hollway's Norway. 2*s*.
Maurel's Wellington. 1*s*. 6*d*.
Campbell's Life of Bacon. 2*s*. 6*d*.
The Flower Garden. 1*s*.
Taylor's Notes from Life. 2*s*.
Rejected Addresses. 1*s*.
Penn's Hints on Angling. 1*s*.

MUSTERS' (Capt.) At Home with the Patagonians; a Year's Wanderings over Untrodden Ground from the Straits of Magellan to the Rio Negro. *2nd Edition.* Illustrations. Post 8vo.

NAPIER'S (Sir Chas.) Life, Journals, and Letters. By Sir W. Napier. *Second Edition.* Portraits. 4 Vols. Post 8vo. 48*s*.

———— (Sir Wm.) Life and Letters. Edited by Rt. Hon. H. A. Bruce. Portraits. 2 Vols. Crown 8vo. 28*s*.

———— English Battles and Sieges of the Peninsular War. *Fourth Edition.* Portrait. Post 8vo. 9*s*.

NAPOLEON AT FONTAINEBLEAU AND ELBA. A Journal of Occurrences and Notes of Conversations. By Sir Neil Campbell, C.B., British Commissioner. With a Memoir of that Officer By Rev. A. N. C. Maclachlan, M.A. Portrait. 8vo. 15*s*.

NAUTICAL (The) ALMANAC. Royal 8vo. 2*s*. 6*d*. (*By Authority.*)

NAVY LIST. Monthly, 1*s*. 6*d*. and Quarterly, 3*s*. Post 8vo. (*By Authority.*)

NEW TESTAMENT. With Short Explanatory Commentary. By Archdeacon Churton, M.A., and Archdeacon Basil Jones, M.A. With 110 authentic Views, &c. 2 Vols. Crown 8vo. 21*s*. *bound.*

NICHOLLS' (Sir George) History of the English, Irish and Scotch Poor Laws. 4 Vols. 8vo.

NICOLAS' (Sir Harris) Historic Peerage of England. Exhibiting the Origin, Descent, and Present State of every Title of Peerage which has existed in this Country since the Conquest. By William Courthope. 8vo. 30*s*.

NIMROD, On the Chace—Turf—and Road. With Portrait by Maclise and Plates by Alken. Crown 8vo. 5*s*. Or with Coloured Plates, 7*s*. 6*d*.

OLD LONDON; Papers read at the Archæological Institute. By various Authors. 8vo. 12*s*.

ORMATHWAITE'S (Lord) Astronomy and Geology—Darwin and Buckle—Progress and Civilisation. Crown 8vo. 6*s*.

OWEN'S (Lieut.-Col.) Principles and Practice of Modern Artillery, including Artillery Material, Gunnery, and Organisation and Use of Artillery in Warfare. *Second Edition.* With Illustrations. 8vo. 15*s*.

OXENHAM'S (Rev. W.) English Notes for Latin Elegiacs; designed for early Proficients in the Art of Latin Versification, with Prefatory Rules of Composition in Elegiac Metre. *Fourth Edition.* 12mo. 3*s*. 6*d*.

PALGRAVE'S (R. H. J.) Local Taxation of Great Britain and Ireland. 8vo. 5*s*.

PALLISER'S (Mrs.) Brittany and its Byeways, its Inhabitants, and Antiquities. With Illustrations. Post 8vo. 12*s*.

———— Mottoes for Monuments, or Epitaphs selected for General Use and Study. With Illustrations. Crown 8vo. 7*s*. 6*d*.

PARIS' (DR.) Philosophy in Sport made Science in Earnest; or, the First Principles of Natural Philosophy inculcated by aid of the Toys and Sports of Youth. *Ninth Edition.* Woodcuts. Post 8vo. 7s. 6d.

PARKMAN'S (FRANCIS) Discovery of the Great West; or, the Valleys of the Mississippi and the Lakes of North America. An Historical Narrative. Map. 8vo. 10s. 6d.

PARKYNS' (MANSFIELD) Three Years' Residence in Abyssinia: with Travels in that Country. *Second Edition,* with Illustrations. Post 8vo. 7s. 6d.

PEEL'S (SIR ROBERT) Memoirs. Edited by EARL STANHOPE and Mr. CARDWELL. 2 Vols. Post 8vo. 7s. 6d. each.

PENN'S (RICHARD) Maxims and Hints for an Angler and Chess-player. Woodcuts. Fcap. 8vo. 1s.

PERCY'S (JOHN, M.D.) Metallurgy. Vol. I. Fuel, Coal, Fire-Clays, Copper, Zinc, Brass, &c. *New Edition.* With Illustrations. 8vo. (*Nearly ready.*)

——— Vol. II. Iron and Steel. *New Edition.* With Illustrations. 8vo. (*In preparation.*)

——— Vol. III. Lead, including Desilverization and Cupellation. With Illustrations. 8vo. 30s.

——— Metallurgy. Vols. IV. and V. Gold, Silver, and Mercury, Platinum, Tin, Nickel, Cobalt, Antimony, Bismuth, Arsenic, and other Metals. With Illustrations. 8vo. (*In Preparation.*)

PHILLIPS' (JOHN) Memoirs of William Smith. 8vo. 7s. 6d.

——— Geology of Yorkshire, The Coast, and Limestone District. Plates. 4to. Part I., 20s.—Part II., 30s.

——— Rivers, Mountains, and Sea Coast of Yorkshire. With Essays on the Climate, Scenery, and Ancient Inhabitants. *Second Edition,* Plates. 8vo. 15s.

PHILPOTTS' (BISHOP) Letters to the late Charles Butler, on his "Book of the Roman Catholic Church." *New Edition.* Post 8vo. 6s.

PICK'S (DR.) Popular Etymological Dictionary of the French Language. 8vo. 7s. 6d.

POPE'S (ALEXANDER) Works. With Introductions and Notes, by REV. WHITWELL ELWIN. Vols. I., II., VI., VII., VIII. With Portraits. 8vo. 10s. 6d. each.

PORTER'S (REV. J. L.) Damascus, Palmyra and Lebanon. With Travels among the Giant Cities of Bashan and the Hauran. *New Edition.* Map and Woodcuts. Post 8vo. 7s. 6d.

PRAYER-BOOK (ILLUSTRATED), with Borders, Initials, Vignettes, &c. Edited, with Notes, by REV. THOS. JAMES. Medium 8vo. 18s. *cloth*; 31s. 6 d. *calf*; 36s. *morocco.*

PUSS IN BOOTS. With 12 Illustrations. By OTTO SPECKTER. 16mo. 1s. 6d. Or coloured, 2s. 6d.

PRINCIPLES AT STAKE. Essays on Church Questions of the Day. 8vo. 12s. Contents:—

Ritualism and Uniformity.—Benjamin Shaw.
The Episcopate.—Bishop of Bath and Wells.
The Priesthood.—Dean of Canterbury.
National Education.—Rev. Alexander R. Grant.
Doctrine of the Eucharist.—Rev. G. H. Sumner.
Scripture and Ritual.—Canon Bernard.
Church in South Africa.—Arthur Mills.
Schismatical Tendency of Ritualism.—Rev. Dr. Salmon.
Revisions of the Liturgy.—Rev. W. G. Humphry.
Parties and Party Spirit.—Dean of Chester.

QUARTERLY REVIEW (The). 8vo. 6s.

RAMBLES in the Syrian Deserts. Post 8vo. 10s. 6d.

RANKE'S (Leopold) History of the Popes of Rome during the 16th and 17th Centuries. Translated from the German by Sarah Austin. *Third Edition.* 3 Vols. 8vo. 30s.

RASSAM'S (Hormuzd) Narrative of the British Mission to Abyssinia. With Notices of the Countries Traversed from Massowah to Magdala. Illustrations. 2 Vols. 8vo. 28s.

RAWLINSON'S (Rev. George) Herodotus. A New English Version. Edited with Notes and Essays. *Second Edition.* Maps and Woodcut. 4 Vols. 8vo. 48s.

——— Five Great Monarchies of Chaldæa, Assyria, Media, Babylonia, and Persia. *Second Edition.* With Maps and Illustrations. 3 Vols. 8vo. 42s.

REED'S (E. J.) Shipbuilding in Iron and Steel; a Practical Treatise, giving full details of Construction, Processes of Manufacture, and Building Arrangements. With 5 Plans and 250 Woodcuts. 8vo. 30s.

——— Iron-Clad Ships; their Qualities, Performances, and Cost. With Chapters on Turret Ships, Iron-Clad Rams, &c. With Illustrations. 8vo. 12s.

REJECTED ADDRESSES (The). By James and Horace Smith. *New Edition.* Woodcuts. Post 8vo. 3s. 6d.; or *Cheap Edition*, Fcap. 8vo. 1s.

RENNIE'S (D. F.) British Arms in Peking, 1860. Post 8vo. 12s.

——— Narrative of the British Embassy in China. Illustrations. 2 Vols. Post 8vo. 24s.

——— Story of Bhotan and the Dooar War. Map and Woodcut. Post 8vo. 12s.

RESIDENCE IN BULGARIA; or, Notes on the Resources and Administration of Turkey, &c. By S. G. B. St. Clair and Charles A. Brophy. 8vo. 12s.

REYNOLDS' (Sir Joshua) Life and Times. By C. R. Leslie, R.A. and Tom Taylor. Portraits. 2 Vols. 8vo.

RICARDO'S (David) Political Works. With a Notice of his Life and Writings. By J. R. M'Culloch. *New Edition.* 8vo. 16s.

RIPA'S (Father) Thirteen Years' Residence at the Court of Peking. Post 8vo. 2s.

ROBERTSON'S (Canon) History of the Christian Church, from the Apostolic Age to the end of the Fifth Council of the Lateran, 1517. 4 Vols. 8vo.

The Work may be had separately.

Vol. 1.—A.D. 64-590. 8vo. 18s.
Vol. 2.—A.D. 590-1122. 8vo. 20s.
Vol. 3.—A.D. 1122-1303. 8vo. 18s.
Vol. 4.—A.D. 1303-1517. 8vo.

——— How shall we Conform to the Liturgy of the Church of England? *Third Edition.* Post 8vo. 9s.

ROME. *See* Liddell and Smith.

ROWLAND'S (David) Manual of the English Constitution; Its Rise, Growth, and Present State. Post 8vo. 10s. 6d.

——— Laws of Nature the Foundation of Morals. Post 8vo. 6s.

RUNDELL'S (MRS.) Modern Domestic Cookery. Woodcuts. Fcap. 8vo. 5*s.*

RUXTON'S (GEORGE F.) Travels in Mexico; with Adventures among the Wild Tribes and Animals of the Prairies and Rocky Mountains. Post 8vo. 3*s.* 6*d.*

ROBINSON'S (REV. DR.) Biblical Researches in Palestine and the Adjacent Regions, 1838—52. *Third Edition.* Maps. 3 Vols. 8 vo. 42*s.*

——— Physical Geography of the Holy Land. Post 8vo. 10*s.* 6*d.*

——— (WM.) Alpine Flowers for English Gardens. With 70 Illustrations. Crown 8vo. 12*s.*

——— Wild Garden; or, our Groves and Shrubberies made beautiful by the Naturalization of Hardy Exotic Plants. With Frontispiece. Small 8vo. 6*s.*

——— Sub-Tropical Garden; or, Beauty of Form in the Flower Garden. With Illustrations. Small 8vo. 7*s.* 6*d.*

SALE'S (SIR ROBERT) Brigade in Affghanistan. With an Account of the Defence of Jellalabad. By REV. G. R. GLEIG. Post 8vo. 2*s.*

SALLESBURY'S (EDWARD) "Children of the Lake." A Poem. Fcap. 8vo. 4*s.* 6*d.*

SCOTT'S (SIR G. G.) Secular and Domestic Architecture, Present and Future. 8vo. 9*s.*

——— Rise and Development of Mediæval Architecture. 8vo. (*Nearly Ready.*)

——— (DEAN) University Sermons. Post 8vo. 8*s.* 6*d.*

SCROPE'S (G. P.) Geology and Extinct Volcanoes of Central France. Illustrations. Medium 8vo. 30*s.*

SHAW'S (T. B.) Manual of English Literature. Edited, with Notes and Illustrations. Post 8vo. 7*s.* 6*d.*

——— Specimens of English Literature. Selected from the Chief Writers. Post 8vo. 7*s.* 6*d.*

——— (ROBERT) Visit to High Tartary, Yarkand, and Kashgar (formerly Chinese Tartary), and Return Journey over the Karakorum Pass. With Map and Illustrations. 8vo. 16*s.*

SMILES' (SAMUEL) Lives of British Engineers; from the Earliest Period. With 9 Portraits and 400 Illustrations. 4 Vols. 8vo. 21*s.* each.

——— Lives of George and Robert Stephenson. With Portraits and Illustrations. Medium 8vo. 21*s.* Or *Popular Edition*, with Woodcuts. Post 8vo. 6*s.*

——— Lives of Boulton and Watt. With Portraits and Illustrations. Medium 8vo. 21*s.*

——— Self-Help. With Illustrations of Conduct and Perseverance. Post 8vo. 6*s* Or in French. 5*s.*

——— Character. A Companion Volume to "SELF-HELP." Post 8vo. 6*s.*

——— Industrial Biography: Iron-Workers and Tool Makers. Post 8vo. 6*s.*

——— Lives of Brindley and the Early Engineers. With Portrait and 50 Woodcuts. Post 8vo. 6*s.*

——— Life of Thomas Telford. With a History of Roads and Travelling in England. Woodcuts. Post 8vo. 6*s.*

——— Huguenots in England and Ireland: their Settlements, Churches and Industries. *Third Edition.* Post 8vo. 6*s.*

——— Boy's Voyage round the World; including a Residence in Victoria, and a Journey by Rail across North America. With Illustrations. Post 8vo. 6*s.*

SHIRLEY (Evelyn P.) on Deer and Deer Parks, or some Account of English Parks, with Notes on the Management of Deer. Illustrations. 4to. 21*s.*

SIERRA LEONE; Described in Letters to Friends at Home. By A Lady. Post 8vo. 3*s.* 6*d.*

SIMMONS (Capt. T. F.) on the Constitution and Practice of Courts-Martial; with a Summary of the Law of Evidence, and some Notice of the Criminal Law of England with reference to the Trial of Civil Offences. *Sixth Edition.* 8vo.

STANLEY'S (Dean) Sinai and Palestine. Map. 8vo. 14*s.*

——— Bible in the Holy Land; Extracted from the above Work. By a Lady. Woodcuts. Fcap. 8vo. 2*s.* 6*d.*

——— St. Paul's Epistles to the Corinthians. With Dissertations and Notes. 8vo. 18*s.*

——— History of the Eastern Church. Plans. 8vo. 12*s.*

——— Jewish Church. *Third Edition.* 2 Vols. 8vo. 24*s.*

——— Church of Scotland. 8vo. 7*s.* 6*d.*

——— Historical Memorials of Canterbury Cathedral. *Fifth Edition.* Woodcuts. Post 8vo. 7*s.* 6*d.*

——— Westminster Abbey. *Third Edition.* With Illustrations. 8vo. 21*s.*

——— Sermons in the East, during a Tour with the Prince of Wales. 8vo. 9*s.*

——— on Evangelical and Apostolical Teaching. Post 8vo. 7*s.* 6*d.*

——— Addresses and Charges of Bishop Stanley. With Memoir. 8vo. 10*s.* 6*d.*

SMITH'S (Dr. Wm.) Dictionary of the Bible; its Antiquities, Biography, Geography, and Natural History. Illustrations. 3 Vols. 8vo. 105*s.*

——— Concise Dictionary of the Bible. With 300 Illustrations. Medium 8vo. 21*s.*

——— Smaller Dictionary of the Bible. With Illustrations. Post 8vo. 7*s.* 6*d.*

——— Historical Atlas of Ancient Geography—Biblical and Classical. (5 Parts.) Parts I. and II. Folio. 21*s.* each.

——— Greek and Roman Antiquities. With 500 Illustrations. Medium 8vo. 28*s.*

——— Biography and Mythology With 600 Illustrations. 3 Vols. Medium 8vo. 4*l.* 4*s*

——— Geography. 2 Vols. With 500 Illustrations. Medium 8vo. 56*s.*

——— Classical Dictionary of Mythology, Biography, and Geography. 1 Vol. With 750 Woodcuts. 8vo. 18*s.*

——— Smaller Classical Dictionary. With 200 Woodcuts. Crown 8vo. 7*s.* 6*d.*

——— Greek and Roman Antiquities. With 200 Woodcuts. Crown 8vo. 7*s.* 6*d.*

——— Latin English Dictionary. With Tables of the Roman Calendar, Measures, Weights, and Money. Medium 8vo. 21*s.*

——— Smaller Latin-English Dictionary. 12mo. 7*s.* 6*d.*

——— English-Latin Dictionary. Medium 8vo. 21*s.*

——— Smaller English-Latin Dictionary. 12mo. 7*s.* 6*d.*

SMITH'S (Dr. Wm.) School Manual of English Grammar, with Copious Exercises. Post 8vo. 3*s.* 6*d.*

——— Primary English Grammar. 16mo.

——— History of Britain. 12mo. 2*s.* 6*d.*

——— Principia Latina—Part I. A Grammar, Delectus, and Exercise Book, with Vocabularies. With the ACCIDENCE arranged for the "Public School Primer." 12mo. 3*s.* 6*d.*

——— Part II. A Reading-book of Mythology, Geography, Roman Antiquities, and History. With Notes and Dictionary. 12mo. 3*s.* 6*d.*

——— Part III. A Latin Poetry Book. Hexameters and Pentameters; Eclog. Ovidianæ; Latin Prosody. 12mo. 3*s.* 6*d.*

——— Part IV. Latin Prose Composition. Rules of Syntax, with Examples, Explanations of Synonyms, and Exercises on the Syntax. 12mo. 3*s.* 6*d.*

——— Part V. Short Tales and Anecdotes for Translation into Latin. 12mo. 3*s.*

——— Latin-English Vocabulary and First Latin-English Dictionary for Phædrus, Cornelius Nepos, and Cæsar. 12mo. 3*s.* 6*d.*

——— Student's Latin Grammar. Post 8vo. 6*s.*

——— Smaller Latin Grammar. 12mo. 3*s.* 6*d.*

——— Initia Græca, Part I. An Introduction to Greek; comprehending Grammar, Delectus, and Exercise-book. With Vocabularies. 12mo. 3*s.* 6*d.*

——— Initia Græca, Part II. A Reading Book. Containing Short Tales, Anecdotes, Fables, Mythology, and Grecian History. 12mo. 3*s.* 6*d.*

——— Initia Græca, Part III. Greek Prose Composition. Containing the Rules of Syntax, with copious Examples and Exercises. 12mo. 3*s.* 6*d.*

——— Student's Greek Grammar. By PROFESSOR CURTIUS. Post 8vo. 6*s.*

——— Smaller Greek Grammar. 12mo. 3*s.* 6*d.*

——— Greek Accidence, extracted from the above work. 12mo. 2*s.* 6*d.*

——— Smaller History of England. Woodcuts. 16mo. 3*s.* 6*d.*

——— History of Greece. Woodcuts. 16mo. 3*s.* 6*d.*

——— History of Rome. Woodcuts. 16mo. 3*s.* 6*d.*

——— Classical Mythology. With Translations from the Poets. Woodcuts. 16mo. 3*s.* 6*d.*

——— History of English Literature. 16mo. 3*s.* 6*d.*

——— Specimens of English Literature. 16mo. 3*s.* 6*d.*

——— Scripture History. Woodcuts. 16mo. 3*s.* 6*d.*

——— Ancient History of the East. Woodcuts. 16mo. 3*s.* 6*d.*

——— Geography. Woodcuts. 16mo. 3*s.* 6*d.*

——— (PHILIP) History of the Ancient World, from the Creation to the Fall of the Roman Empire, A.D. 455. *Fourth Edition.* 3 Vols. 8vo. 31*s.* 6*d.*

——— (REV. A. C.) Attractions of the Nile and its Banks. Woodcuts. 2 Vols. Post 8vo. 18*s.*

STUDENT'S HUME. A History of England from the Invasion of Julius Cæsar. By DAVID HUME. Continued to 1868. Woodcuts. Post 8vo. *7s. 6d.*

*** Questions on the above Work, 12mo. 2s.

——— HISTORY OF FRANCE; from the Earliest Times to the Establishment of the Second Empire, 1852. By REV. H. W. JERVIS. Woodcuts. Post 8vo. *7s. 6d.*

——— HISTORY OF ROME; from the Earliest Times to the Establishment of the Empire. By DEAN LIDDELL. Woodcuts. Crown 8vo. *7s. 6d.*

——— GIBBON; an Epitome of the Decline and Fall of the Roman Empire. Woodcuts. Post 8vo. *7s. 6d.*

——— HISTORY OF GREECE; from the Earliest Times to the Roman Conquest. By WM. SMITH, D.C.L. Woodcuts. Crown 8vo. *7s. 6d.*

*** Questions on the above Work, 12mo. *2s.*

——— ANCIENT HISTORY OF THE EAST; Egypt, Assyria, Babylonia, Media, Persia, Asia Minor, and Phœnicia. By PHILIP SMITH. Woodcuts. Post 8vo. *7s. 6d.*

——— OLD TESTAMENT HISTORY; from the Creation to the Return of the Jews from Captivity. Maps and Woodcuts. Post 8vo. *7s. 6d.*

——— NEW TESTAMENT HISTORY. With an Introduction connecting the History of the Old and New Testaments. Maps and Woodcuts. Post 8vo. *7s. 6d.*

——— ANCIENT GEOGRAPHY. By REV. W. L. BEVAN. Woodcuts. Post 8vo. *7s. 6d.*

——— MODERN GEOGRAPHY; Mathematical, Physical, and Descriptive. By REV. W. L. BEVAN. Woodcuts. Post 8vo. *7s. 6d.*

——— ENGLISH LANGUAGE. By GEO. P. MARSH. Post 8vo. *7s. 6d.*

——— LITERATURE. By T. B. SHAW, M.A. Post 8vo. *7s. 6d.*

——— SPECIMENS of English Literature from the Chief Writers. By T. B. SHAW, Post 8vo. *7s. 6d.*

——— MORAL PHILOSOPHY. By WILLIAM FLEMING, D.D. Post 8vo. *7s. 6d.*

——— BLACKSTONE. By R. MALCOLM KERR, LL.D. Post 8vo. *7s. 6d.*

SPALDING'S (CAPTAIN) Tale of Frithiof. Translated from the Swedish of ESIAS TEGNER. Post 8vo. *7s. 6d.*

STEPHEN'S (REV. W. R.) Life and Times of St. Chrysostom. With Portrait. 8vo. *15s.*

ST. CLAIR and BROPHY'S RESIDENCE IN BULGARIA; or, Notes on the Resources and Administration of Turkey. 8vo. *12s.*

ST. JOHN'S (CHARLES) Wild Sports and Natural History of the Highlands. Post 8vo. *3s. 6d.*

——— (BAYLE) Adventures in the Libyan Desert. Post 8vo. *2s.*

STORIES FOR DARLINGS. With Illustrations. Sq. 16mo. *5s.*

STOTHARD'S (THOS.) Life. With Personal Reminiscences. By MRS. BRAY. With Portrait and 60 Woodcuts. 4to. *21s.*

STREET'S (G. E.) Gothic Architecture in Spain. *Second Edition.* With Illustrations. Medium 8vo. *30s.*

STANHOPE'S (EARL) Reign of Queen Anne until the Peace of Utrecht. 1701—13. *Library Edition.* 8vo. 16s. *Cabinet Edition.* With Portrait, 2 Vols. Post 8vo. 10s.

——— History of England, from the Peace of Utrecht to the Peace of Versailles, 1713-83. *Library Edition.* 7 vols. 8vo. 93s. Or, *Cabinet Edition*, 7 vols. Post 8vo. 5s. each.

——— British India, from its Origin to 1783. P. 8vo. 3s. 6d.

——— History of "Forty-Five." Post 8vo. 3s.

——— Spain under Charles the Second. Post 8vo. 6s. 6d.

——— Historical and Critical Essays. Post 8vo. 3s. 6d.

——— Life of Belisarius. Post 8vo. 10s. 6d.

——— ——— Condé. Post 8vo. 3s. 6d.

——— ——— William Pitt. Portraits. 4 Vols. P. 8vo. 24s.

——— Miscellanies. 2 Vols. Post 8vo. 13s.

——— Story of Joan of Arc. Fcap. 8vo. 1s.

STYFFE (KNUTT) On the Strength of Iron and Steel. Translated by C. P. SANDBERG. With Preface by DR. PERCY. With Plates. 8vo. 12s.

SOMERVILLE'S (MARY) Physical Geography. *Sixth Edition, Revised.* By W. H. BATES. Portrait. Post 8vo. 9s.

——— Connexion of the Physical Sciences. *Ninth Edition.* Woodcuts. Post 8vo. 9s.

——— Molecular and Microscopic Science. Illustrations. 2 Vols. Post 8vo. 21s.

——— Personal Recollections from Early Life to Advanced Age. Crown 8vo. *(In Preparation.)*

SOUTH'S (JOHN F.) Household Surgery; or, Hints on Emergencies. Woodcuts. Fcp. 8vo. 4s. 6d.

SOUTHEY'S (ROBERT) Book of the Church. Post 8vo. 7s. 6d.

——— Lives of Bunyan and Cromwell. Post 8vo. 2s.

SYBEL'S (VON) History of Europe during the French Revolution, 1789—1795. 4 Vols. 8vo. 48s.

SYMONDS' (REV. W.) Records of the Rocks; or Notes on the Geology, Natural History, and Antiquities of North and South Wales, Siluria, Devon, and Cornwall. With Illustrations. Crown 8vo. 12s.

TAYLOR'S (SIR HENRY) Notes from Life. Fcap. 8vo. 2s.

THOMS' (W. J.) Longevity of Man; its Facts and its Fiction. Including Observations on the more Remarkable Instances. Post 8vo.

THOMSON'S (ARCHBISHOP) Lincoln's Inn Sermons. 8vo. 10s. 6d.

——— Life in the Light of God's Word. Post 8vo. 5s.

TOCQUEVILLE'S (M. DE) State of France before the Revolution, 1789. Translated by HENRY REEVE. 2nd *Edition*. 8vo.

TOZER'S (H. F.) Highlands of Turkey, with Visits to Mounts Ida, Athos, Olympus, and Pelion. Illustrations. 2 Vols. Crown 8vo. 24s.

TRISTRAM'S (CANON) Great Sahara. Illustrations. Post 8vo. 15s.

——— Land of Moab; Travels on the East side of the Dead Sea and the Jordan. Illustrations. Crown 8vo.

TWISS' (HORACE) Life of Lord Eldon. 2 Vols. Post 8vo. 21s.

TYLOR'S (E. B.) Early History of Mankind, and the Development of Civilization. *Second Edition.* 8vo. 12s.

——— Primitive Culture; the Development of Mythology, Philosophy, Religion, Art, and Custom. 2 Vols. 8vo. 24s.

VAMBERY'S (ARMINIUS) Travels from Teheran across the Turkoman Desert on the Eastern Shore of the Caspian. Illustrations. 8vo. 21*s.*

VAN LENNEP'S (HENRY J.) Travels in Asia Minor. With Illustrations of Biblical Literature, and Archæology. With Woodcuts. 2 Vols. Post 8vo. 24*s.*

WELLINGTON'S Despatches; during his Campaigns in India, Denmark, Portugal, Spain, the Low Countries, and France. Compiled by COLONEL GURWOOD, C.B. 8 Vols. 8vo. 20*s.* each.

——— Supplementary Despatches, relating to India, Ireland, Denmark, Spanish America, Spain, Portugal, France, Congress of Vienna, Waterloo and Paris. Edited by his SON. 14 Vols. 8vo. 20*s.* each.

——— *** An Index to the Despatches. 8vo. 20*s.*

——— Civil and Political Correspondence. Edited by his SON. Vols. I. to IV. 8vo. 20*s.* each.

——— Selections from Despatches. 8vo. 18*s.*

——— Speeches in Parliament. 2 Vols. 8vo. 42*s.*

WHEELER'S (G.) Choice of a Dwelling; a Practical Handbook of Useful Information on all Points connected with Hiring, Buying, or Building a House. *Third Edition.* Plans. Post 8vo. 7*s.* 6*d.*

WHITE'S (HENRY) Massacre of St. Bartholomew. Based on Documents in the Archives of France. 8vo. 16*s.*

WHYMPER'S (EDWARD) Scrambles among the Alps. With the First Ascent of the Matterhorn, and Notes on Glacial Phenomena. *Second Edition.* With 100 Illustrations. 8vo. 21*s.*

——— (FREDERICK) Travels and Adventures in Alaska and on the River Yukon. With Illustrations. 8vo. 16*s.*

WILBERFORCE'S (WILLIAM) Life. By his Son, the BISHOP OF WINCHESTER. Portrait. Post 8vo. 6*s.*

WILKINSON'S (SIR J. G.) Popular Account of the Ancient Egyptians. With 500 Woodcuts. 2 Vols. Post 8vo. 12*s.*

WOOD'S (CAPTAIN) Journey to the Source of the Oxus. *New Edition.* With an Essay on the Geography of the Valley of the Oxus. By COLONEL HENRY YULE, C.C. With Map. 8vo. 12*s.*

WORDSWORTH'S (BISHOP OF LINCOLN) Athens and Attica. *Fourth Edition.* Plates. Post 8vo. 5*s.*

——— Pictorial, Descriptive, and Historical Account of Greece. *New Edition.* With 600 Woodcuts. Royal 8vo. 21*s.*

YULE'S (COLONEL) Book of Marco Polo, concerning the Kingdoms and Marvels of the East. A new English Version. Illustrated by the Light of Oriental Writers and Modern Travels. With Maps and 80 Plates. 2 Vols. Medium 8vo. 42*s.*

ZINCKE'S (REV. F. B.) Winter in the United States. Post 8vo. 10*s.* 6*d.*